THE ESSENTIAL BERKELEY AND NEO-BERKELEY

ALSO AVAILABLE FROM BLOOMSBURY

Berkeley and Irish Philosophy, David Berman
The Bloomsbury Companion to Berkeley,
ed. Bertil Belfrage and Richard Brook
The Bloomsbury Companion to Locke, ed. S.-J. Savonius-Wroth,
Paul Schuurman and Jonathan Walmsley
The Bloomsbury Companion to Hume,
ed. Alan Bailey and Dan O'Brien

THE ESSENTIAL
BERKELEY AND
NEO-BERKELEY

DAVID BERMAN

BLOOMSBURY ACADEMIC
LONDON • NEW YORK • OXFORD • NEW DELHI • SYDNEY

BLOOMSBURY ACADEMIC
Bloomsbury Publishing Plc
50 Bedford Square, London, WC1B 3DP, UK
1385 Broadway, New York, NY 10018, USA
29 Earlsfort Terrace, Dublin 2, Ireland

BLOOMSBURY, BLOOMSBURY ACADEMIC and the Diana logo
are trademarks of Bloomsbury Publishing Plc

First published in Great Britain 2022

Cover design by Ben Anslow.
Cover images: George Berkeley (1685–1753) Anglo-Irish philosopher aka Bishop
Berkeley (© Pictorial Press Ltd / Alamy); George Berkeley (1685–1753),
aka Bishop Berkeley (Bishop of Cloyne). Anglo-Irish philosopher. Vanderbank
(© Classic Image / Alamy); A vertical oval ornate decorative hand carved natural
wooden frame (© Image Farm Inc. / Alamy); A vertical gold thin decorative
ornate oval antique frame (© Image Farm Inc. / Alamy)

Bloomsbury Publishing Plc does not have any control over, or
responsibility for, any third-party websites referred to or in this book.
All internet addresses given in this book were correct at the time of
going to press. The author and publisher regret any inconvenience
caused if addresses have changed or sites have ceased to exist,
but can accept no responsibility for any such changes.

A catalogue record for this book is available from the British Library.

Library of Congress Cataloging-in-Publication Data.
Names: Berman, David, 1942- author.
Title: The essential Berkeley and Neo-Berkeley / David Berman.
Description: London ; New York : Bloomsbury Academic, 2022. |
Includes bibliographical references and index.
Identifiers: LCCN 2021035912 (print) | LCCN 2021035913 (ebook) |
ISBN 9781350214729 (pb) | ISBN 9781350214712 (hb) |
ISBN 9781350214736 (epdf) | ISBN 9781350214743 (ebook)
Subjects: LCSH: Berkeley, George, 1685–1753.
Classification: LCC B1348 .B459 2022 (print) | LCC B1348 (ebook) | DDC 192–dc23
LC record available at https://lccn.loc.gov/2021035912
LC ebook record available at https://lccn.loc.gov/2021035913

ISBN: HB: 978-1-3502-1471-2
           PB: 978-1-3502-1472-9
           ePDF: 978-1-3502-1473-6
           eBook: 978-1-3502-1474-3

Typeset by Integra Software Services Pvt. Ltd.
Printed and bound in Great Britain

To find out more about our authors and books visit www.bloomsbury.com
and sign up for our newsletters.

CONTENTS

PREFACE

This book has two parts, each divided into sections. Part one is mainly exegetical and focuses on Berkeley's writings, which I look at in a chronological way, in accordance with his own wish (as expressed in his letter of 24 March 1730) 'that all the things I have published on these philosophical subjects were read in the order wherein I published them'. In this part, I maintain that what is essential to his philosophy is not his immaterialism or idealism, as is usually thought, but his dualism.

In part two I move from exegesis to what I believe to be the truth. So here I move from Berkeley to Neo-Berkeley. For many present-day philosophy teachers, Berkeley is seen as little more than an important transition from Locke to Hume, and probably the least significant of the three great British Empiricists. So Berkeleianism has become more a museum-piece than a living philosophy, which is very different from how it was seen in the nineteenth century, the great age of idealism. However, as I try to show here,

Berkeley's philosophy can become a living force once again. How? Very briefly, by taking seriously his essential dualism, then taking it further than he took it, by shedding his monotheistic God, as well as his notional understanding and defense of dualism in favour of one based on experience. For in this way, I believe it can be shown that Berkeley's essential and now enlarged dualism is not defeated by Hume's phenomenalist criticism of mind, as it is according to the usual way of seeing the history of philosophy.

For convenience, I talk in part one but especially in part two of 'Neo-Berkeley', who is virtually the same as myself, David Berman, the writer of this work. But just as Berkeley introduced Philonous, in his *Three Dialogues*, to speak clearly and directly for him, so I have introduced Neo-Berkeley to speak for me. He is my ideal spokesperson. For unlike me, Neo-Berkeley's primary concern is attaining and presenting the truth, not understanding Berkeley. So while I think Berkeley went very far in getting to the truth, I think on some matters he was mistaken, and that on others it is not clear what he held. The latter, unfortunately, are on some of the most important matters. But even if it proves that in these problematic matters he was mistaken, they might still be valuable as coming close to the truth. But what, it might be asked, is coming close to the truth? Whatever it is, I think it is likely to make things confusing. And partly to avoid this confusion, I have introduced Neo-Berkeley. For while I, DB, am also concerned to get to the truth, I also want to understand Berkeley's actual philosophy. So unlike Neo-Berkeley, I can sometimes get too involved in scholarly matters, whereas he is more rigorous in cutting to the chase, and ignoring what Berkeley held if it is not clear and justified. And yet, like me, Neo-Berkeley nonetheless considers himself Berkeleian. For he realizes that if there was no actual Berkeley, then there would have been no Neo-Berkeley. And this can be seen in the longest section of part two, section 7, where Neo-B's Visual Tactual Typology is presented.

.....

This book draws on my three published books on Berkeley – *Berkeley: Idealism and the Man* (1994); *Berkeley and Experimental Philosophy* (1997) and *Berkeley and Irish Philosophy* (2005) – and can be considered the culmination of my scholarly work on Berkeley over the past fifty years.

An early version of the present work was used as the primary text for a fourth-year research seminar at

Trinity College Dublin, taught by Prof. Vasilis Politis and myself in 2014. I am grateful to him and those attending the course for helpful discussion. I am also grateful to Dr Laura Kennedy for reading and commenting an early version of this work, to Vincent Denard for translating the quotations from Berkeley's *De Motu* used in this work, and to Prof James Hill for many valuable discussions on various topics relating to this work.

… … ….

ABBREVIATIONS

cde=   core dualistic experience
Neo-B=   Neo-Berkeley
TMF=   Typical Mind Fallacy
vt=   visual type
tt=   tactual type
DMT=   Dualist Monist Typology
TVT=   Tactual Visual Typology
TCD=   Trinity College Dublin
s-d=   sense data
Syn=   synaesthesia
De-syn=   eliminating normal syn, which is like nulling an illusion.

… … … …..

Abbreviations of Berkeley's Works:
PCs=   *Philosophical Commentaries*, also called Notebooks
NTV=   *Essay Towards a New Theory of Vision*
Principles
or PHK=   *Principles of Human Knowledge*

DHP= *Three Dialogues between Hylas and Philonous*

Works= *Works of Berkeley,* in 9 volumes, edited by Luce and Jessop

TVV= *Theory of Vision Vindicated*

... ...

PART ONE

BERKELEY'S PHILOSOPHY

Section 1
Overview and summary

Probably the main thesis of this book is that Berkeley's essential philosophical insight, from which the rest of his philosophy unfolds, is the truth of dualism. Simply stated, this is the position that I am a mind that perceives objects, and that what I am is not an object or like any objects. This is Berkeley's dualism. From this, it is possible to go on to summarize his larger philosophy in the following two conclusions: (1) that material objects do not exist and (2) that the space which is left when the fiction of matter is exposed can and should be filled by God, the Infinite Mind, who, according to Berkeley, does what matter was supposed to do, which is to project sensory objects into our minds in an orderly way. This is Berkeley's actual philosophy, sometimes called Immaterialism or Idealism, which I examine especially in part one of this work. My aim is to determine how much of it is justified and which Berkeley should have rejected if he had the benefit of the history of philosophy since his time, so the history of philosophy that includes Hume, Reid, Kant, Hegel, Schopenhauer, Marx, Nietzsche, Bradley, James, Bergson, Husserl, McTaggart, Russell, Wittgenstein and Heidegger, among others.

So just as Berkeley's own philosophy developed at crucial times over the years, especially in 1706–1708 and 1710–1713, then 1732–1734 and finally in 1744–1752, so, I suggest, that if his philosophy is to be a living force, it must grow and develop into a new form which is still Berkeleian but different from what Berkeley accepted in his lifetime. This is what I call Neo-Berkeleian or the philosophy of Neo-Berkeley, which is the main subject of part two, whereas Berkeley's actual philosophy is the subject of part one.

Section 2
Berkeley's life and works

Since the primary aim of this part is to trace the development of Berkeley's actual philosophy, what follows is a brief description of his works in the order in which he wrote them, with some account of what Berkeley was doing when he wrote them.

The first important work is Berkeley's private philosophical notebooks, now generally called the 'Philosophical Commentaries', or PCs, written circa 1706–1707, so in his early twenties, when, as a young Junior Fellow at Trinity College Dublin, he was working out his philosophy. And we can also see him at work in an unpublished work on Infinites, circa 1707, and a draft (circa late 1708) of the Introduction to his *Principles of Human Knowledge*, PHK.

In the next year, 1709, Berkeley published his first major book, *An Essay towards a New Theory of Vision*, 1709, NTV, which is an important work both in philosophy and psychology. More specifically, it aims to prove that we do not know material things by the sense of sight, and it also lays the basis for what Berkeley thought was a new and unanswerable argument for the existence of God.

It was in the following year, however, that Berkeley issued what is generally considered his magnum opus, the *Principles of Human Knowledge*, PHK. This, too, like the NTV, was published in Dublin. As its title page states, it was written 'By George Berkeley, M.A. Fellow of Trinity-College, Dublin', and is Part One. Berkeley never, however, published any further parts. The reception of the PHK was not positive, which Berkeley attributed less to his philosophy than to his presentation; so he decided to cast his PHK in a clearer and more popular form. This is his *Three Dialogues between Hylas and Philonous*, DHP, which as he says in its Preface, he decided to issue, 'before I proceed to the Second Part' of the PHK. The DHP were published in London in 1713, where Berkeley was now living. The DHP is usually considered the next most authoritative statement of his philosophy after the PHK. Of much less importance is Berkeley's work on *Passive Obedience*, which appeared in the previous year, 1712, which is Berkeley's most sustained work of ethical and political philosophy, which had originated as a number of sermons he gave in the Trinity College Chapel.

For the next twenty years, after the DHP, Berkeley would continue to be mostly away from Dublin, either in England, France, Italy or America, although he continued to be a Fellow and sometime teacher on leave from Trinity College until 1724, when he was appointed Dean of Derry, which severed his official link to his College.

In London in 1713, Berkeley quickly became acquainted with some of the great figures of the time, including Alexander Pope, Jonathan Swift and also Sir Richard Steele, formerly the editor of the *Spectator*, now the editor of a new periodical paper, called the *Guardian*, to which Steele asked Berkeley to contribute. Some of his most imaginative ideas are to be found in his *Guardian* essays.

After his 1713 *Guardian* essays, Berkeley published no philosophical works for eight years, during which time he was travelling in France, but especially in Italy, also back to England and Ireland, and working on Part Two of his *Principles*. According to his letter of 10 September 1729, to his American friend, Samuel Johnson, it seems that the manuscript of Part Two of the PHK was lost during his travels in Italy in 1716–1720.

Berkeley's next work in philosophy, after the DHP, was *De Motu*, 1721, which was prompted by the

French Academy's announcement of a prize for the best essay on the subject of motion (which Berkeley's essay did not win).

After *De Motu* there is another long gap in his philosophical output. The explanation is that during most of this time he was pursuing a bold project: the establishment of a missionary-arts college to be located in Bermuda. For this project, he gathered considerable support from both private individuals and the British Government. And to further pursue the project he travelled to America in 1729, where he took up residence in Rhode Island. It was here that he wrote his next and longest book, *Alciphron or the Minute Philosopher*, his main contribution to philosophical theology. *Alciphron* was published in London in 1732, after his return from America and in the wake of the failure of his Bermuda project.

1732–1734 is the next most intense phase of Berkeley's authorship, rivaling that of 1709–1713. Thus after *Alciphron*, Berkeley publishes his *Theory of Vision Vindicated*, TVV, 1733 and, perhaps even more importantly, new editions of the PHK and DHP in 1734, with notable additions, followed by a number of works in the philosophy of mathematics and physics.

After these publications there is another gap, which can be partly explained by Berkeley's new circumstances – his appointment as Bishop of Cloyne in 1734, where he remained until 1752. In this period, 1734–1752, Berkeley's writings are almost exclusively on economic and social matters, the most important of which is his *Querist*, 1735–1737. The conditions in Ireland and especially Cloyne, a remote Cathedral town in Co. Cork, partly explain this turn from philosophical to economic and social matters and also his next publication, *Siris*, 1744, his last and most unusual book, which does in its last part move into philosophy. The initial and probably the main purpose of *Siris* was to recommend a medicine, tar-water, which Berkeley had encountered in America and which he came to believe was of enormous value, which he examines in the early sections of *Siris*. He then in the middle part of the book moves to a wide-ranging discussion of chemistry, biology and physics and then finally in its last part to philosophy and also theology.

Although now generally neglected, *Siris* was his most popular work in his own lifetime, passing through some nine editions, as well as translations into a number of languages, in the next few years. At least initially, tar-water was all the rage in Europe, America and elsewhere and Berkeley was still recommending and supporting tar-water in 1752, when he and his family moved from Cloyne to Oxford.

It was sometime before this move that he delivered in Cloyne what is considered his best sermon. And it was also around this time that he prepared a new edition of *Alciphron* and also a reprint of a number of his earlier pamphlets, including *De Motu*, in a collection called *A Miscellany, containing several tracts on various subjects*. Both the *Miscellany* and *Alciphron* were published in London in 1752. To the *Miscellany* he added one new essay called 'Farther thoughts on tar-water', thus bringing Berkeley's literary career to an end.

Berkeley died in Oxford in January 1753, aged sixty-eight.

Section 3
The structure of Berkeley's *Principles*

Since the *Principles* is the most authoritative statement of Berkeley's philosophy, I think it should be useful if I say a word about its structure. In line with his dualism, Berkeley's PHK is about the two things that exist: objects or ideas and minds or spirits. As we have it, the PHK, as only part one, is very much about objects and proportionately very little about minds, which, from what Berkeley says in his Notebooks, was to be the main subject of part two of the PHK. Thus sections 1, 3–25 are about objects as are most of sections 34–85, which contain Berkeley's self-imposed objections to his immaterialism and his replies to them. This part of the PHK comes to a conclusion in section 86, where he says 'From the principles we have laid down, it follows, human knowledge may naturally be reduced to two heads, that of *ideas* and that of *spirits*. Of each of these I shall treat in order ... '.

This Berkeley does, beginning with objects or ideas in sections 87–134; then moving to spirit in the rest of the work. So of the 156 sections of the body of the PHK, about 120 deal with objects, which leave less than forty sections for his account of spirit or mind, an account which begins with the key section 2, then moves to sections 26–33; and, after a long break, concludes with sections 135–156. Now most of these final twenty-one sections are almost entirely on God and deal with specific theological issues, such as the problem of evil, and do not bear directly on Berkeley's core dualism. However, they do show the dominant role God plays in Berkeley's thinking and also its motivation and tendency, which was to bring his readers to the presence of God, as he earnestly says in section 156. And what Berkeley says is also useful, as I try to show in Part Two, as a model for what I describe as dualistic intimacy between human minds.

Section 4
Berkeley's dualism and dualistic experience

Wittgenstein once said that 'when I read Schopenhauer I seem to see to the bottom very easily. He is not deep in the sense that Kant and Berkeley are deep' (see Drury, p. 158). What Wittgenstein seems to have felt about Berkeley, probably most other readers feel even more: that it is difficult to see to the bottom of his philosophy. Hence my aim in this part is to bring out the hard essential core of his philosophy.

But what then is this core or essential philosophical insight? As mentioned above, it is the truth of dualism, that there are two kinds of basic beings, which for Descartes are minds and material things. This is substance dualism, which Berkeley rejects, since for him material substance is a fiction. But while Berkeley rejects Descartes's substance dualism, Berkeley develops his own form of dualism in the epistemic or perceptual mode.

In short, according to Berkeley, all that exists are minds or perceivers and perceptions or the objects perceived by minds. Each of these things is fundamental yet entirely different, and so irreducible to one another. The objects we perceive are sensory objects, which make up the physical world, but also imaginary objects, formed from sensory objects, and as well as memories. Then there are minds perceiving these objects. Berkeley introduces this dualism straightaway in sections 1 and 2 of his *Principles*. Objects, as he explains, are things such as chairs, stones, cats, which we can, however, experience more directly and immediately in their constituent elements, such as colours, sounds, tastes and smells. For what we perceive as physical things are, according to Berkeley, composed of these simpler sensory objects; and from these objects we can also form or derive other objects, namely mental images.

However, apart from all these objects there is a totally different kind of being, namely, self or mind or spirit, which perceives or thinks or acts about the various objects of the world.

This is crucial and worth repeating: for with these two beings – objects and minds – we have all that exists, according to Berkeley. This is his metaphysics.

So virtually the whole of Berkeley's dualistic metaphysics is clearly set out in the *Principles*, sections 1 and 2, although it is set out in an epistemic mode. This presents a challenge for some present-day philosophers who believe that metaphysics and epistemology need to be distinguished, and that metaphysics has primacy over epistemology. But that is not Berkeley's view, as is shown in his famous formula, 'esse is percipi' (PHK, section 3), which is expanded in his Notebooks, entry number 429, according to which 'esse is percipi or percipere', that is, to be is to be perceived or perceiving, where the primary metaphysical category of being is equated with the primary epistemic category of perception. Hence, to understand Berkeley's metaphysics, we need to recognize that it is epistemological and to understand his epistemology that it is his metaphysics; also that while his metaphysics is dualistic, it is not substance dualism but epistemic or perceptual dualism.

Right from the beginning of the PHK, Berkeley is clear that there are two kinds of objects – those of sense and the images derived from what we sense. But what Berkeley does not tell us until somewhat later in the PHK is that there are also two kinds of minds: finite or human minds and infinite mind, which is

God. Here Berkeley was being somewhat strategic, just as we know he was in the case of matter, that is, in not introducing his distinctive doctrines too early on and too abruptly. So, as he says in a letter of September 1710, to his friend John Percival:

> ... whatever doctrine contradicts vulgar and settled opinion had need been introduced with great caution into the world. For this reason ... I omitted all mention of the non-existence of matter in the title-page [of the PHK] dedication, preface and introduction, that so the notion might steal unawares on the reader.[1]

So Berkeley wanted his two main doctrines to glide gently into the minds of his readers. These are the rejection of matter and its replacement by God.

There is, however, one important instance of unclarity in section 1 of the PHK, which should be mentioned. For here Berkeley seems to say that, apart from sensory objects or images and memories, there is another kind of object, namely 'such as are perceived by attending to the passions and operations of the mind'. Yet while Berkeley seems to be saying that these are objects, it is not clear how they can be objects without breaking down the key division he makes between passive objects and active minds. For operations of the mind seem to be active and go with the mind, not with the objects the mind perceives. And it should also be noted that, unlike the other objects – those of sense, memory and imagination – Berkeley doesn't explicitly describe passions or mental operations as objects, although he does seem to say that we perceive them. However, this takes us into what is probably the most problematic topic in Berkeley's philosophy, namely his attitude to how we know our minds, which I discuss at length below.

With respect to sensory objects, mental images and memories, there is no problem. How do we know these? Berkeley's answer is simple: by experience, that is, by perceiving them; which is why he is generally and, I believe, rightly described as an empiricist. To be sure, Berkeley does distinguish, as mentioned above, between experiencing ordinary things, such as hats and apples, and the sensory constituents of those things. And this is not without its complexities. But the even more vexing problem comes when we turn to minds – although not that there are minds which differ entirely from objects, for that is his essential dualistic insight and truth, clearly stated in section 2 – but how we know minds. That is THE question, and a question which cannot be answered easily or briefly.

That Berkeley wants to say something about this, but is not certain what to say, is probably already being signalled by his ambiguous suggestion in section 1, about the mind's acts and passions as a possible kind of object. For to allow that mental acts are objects would be to break down the very division he insists on in section 2, since minds and their modes of operation are what do the acting, rather than being what is perceived. Thus one apparently simple question, which we shall be addressing below, is: Do I know I am a mind directly or immediately in experience, or indirectly, by inferring it from the objects I perceive or experience and/or produce?

.....

Berkeley uses a number of different names for each of the two basic kinds of things outlined in sections 1 and 2. In section 1, he speaks of objects, which is the term I have been using. But he also speaks of ideas, and then in section 2, he speaks of mind, spirit, soul or my self. I think it is clear that in using these four different names in section 2 he is talking about the same thing, and in what follows I generally use the terms 'mind' or 'self'. But his use of the terms 'objects' and 'ideas' in section 1 is more problematic. For his term 'idea' does tend to mystify readers, even now. Nor was he unaware of its difficulties, for in his Notebooks, entry 807, he seems to regret his decision to use it as his preferred term for what is perceived, and I generally use the term 'object', rather than 'idea'.

Section 5
Dualism or monism?

As my focus in this work is on Berkeley's core dualism, I now need to consider whether Berkeley really is a dualist at all. Tackling this question is necessary, because probably many of those who have attended a general course in the history of philosophy would say that Berkeley was not a dualist. Indeed, they are more likely to regard him as a notable monist, which is probably also the view of many students and readers with just a general interest in philosophy. Yet if one were to ask those with a specialist interest in Berkeley, I do not think they would make the same judgement. At the least, the question would be seen as more problematic; but more likely, I think, most Berkeley specialists would say that, on balance, Berkeley's philosophy was dualistic and not monistic. Thus in my own 1994 book, *George Berkeley: idealist and the man*, I stated that he was a dualist (pp. 60–1, 99), which, as far as I am aware, did not raise a single eyebrow from Berkeley scholars or from reviewers of the book.

However, now after twenty-five years, while I would still (and more confidently) affirm my earlier judgement, I see that the question of Berkeley's dualism is much deeper than I then realized. And yet the key texts that I would now mention to justify my judgement are just the ones I referred to in my earlier book, so especially the opening sections of the PHK, and also *De Motu*.

There are a number of simple ways of understanding why many believe that Berkeley is a monist and could not have been a dualist. Thus everyone agrees that Berkeley believed that matter does not exist. But then, the teachers would say, it follows that there is for Berkeley only one fundamental thing, namely mind. Hence, they would say that Berkeley is a monist, according to which there are only minds and their mental objects. So it seems as simple as that. For how could Berkeley be a dualist if, in his world and his metaphysics, there is no matter or body? And so he is seen, neatly, as the opposite of those, like Hobbes, who is monistic materialist – the opposite being a monistic idealist.

But what those who make this judgement fail to appreciate is that they are assuming that the only valid kind of dualism is substance dualism, so they are imposing an alien grid on Berkeley's philosophy. They also seem to be assuming that matter exists, and that dualism can only be the theory which includes mind and matter, as in substance dualism, so that anyone who denies matter cannot be a dualist.

Why is this line of reasoning mistaken? Because it is not the job of those trying to interpret a philosopher and his philosophy to impose their own philosophical views. Their job is to teach a particular philosophy, in this case Berkeley's, as he understood it. (Of course, they can then go on to criticize it.)

So what did Berkeley himself understand and believe? I think it is abundantly clear from what he says again and again in his works that he believed that there are two basic beings, minds or selves and objects or ideas, and that they are entirely different and irreducible one to the other. Berkeley's texts which state the core dualistic thesis most directly are Notebooks numbers 429, 437 and 672; then PHK, 1710 and 1734, especially sections 1, 2, 89, 139, 141, 142; then the DHP, 1713 and the additions he made to it in 1734; then *De Motu*, especially sections 21, 30; then the TVV, section 11; then *Siris*, sections 290, 292, 294, 296, 297.

Here I take three good examples as representative, apart from the key sections 1 and 2 of PHK, that is, PCs, 437, PHK, section 142 and *De Motu*, section 30:

PC: 437 Impossible any thing Besides that wch thinks & is thought on should exist.

PHK: 142: After what has been said, it is I suppose plain, that our souls are not to be known in the same manner as senseless inactive objects, or by way of *idea. Spirits* and *ideas* are things so wholly different, that when we say, *they exist, they are known*, or the like, these words must not be thought to signify any thing common to both natures. There is nothing alike or common in them …

De Motu: 30: There is given an active res cogitans [thinking substance] which we experience to be a principle of motion in us. This we call soul, mind, spirit; there is given also a res extensa [extended substance] inert, impenetrable, mobile, which differs toto caelo [totally] from the former and constitutes a new genus.

I think it should be clear that these three quotations all capture, although in slightly different ways, the main idea of dualism: that what exists are two totally different kinds of things, known in different ways, which for Berkeley are the passive objects or ideas the mind perceives, and the active mind which perceives them. That Berkeley didn't call himself a dualist or his theory dualistic is irrelevant, since that term was not used by philosophers of his own day. But that he saw himself as what would now be accepted as a dualist is clearly shown by what he says in *De Motu*, where he traces his dualistic ancestry from Anaxagoras, to Socrates and Plato and to Descartes.[2] In short, I think the textual evidence for Berkeley's dualism is clear and overwhelming. Hence going into it in more detail could easily have the effect of dulling what is evident. However, it is probably useful to say something more about the factors that have encouraged the monistic (mis)interpretation. And no doubt one major factor is that it is often thought that Berkeley sees the objects perceived as modes of the mind. And this interpretation is encouraged by his usual term for perceived objects, namely ideas, and also by his claim that all objects or ideas are dependent on and exist in the mind as their substance; also that minds are the only existing substance. And it is true that Berkeley does say in PHK, sections 7 and 135 that mind is the only existing substance (also see PHK section 26). But if, as is usually thought, a substance is something that can exist independently of its modes – as a coffee cup which contains the liquid coffee can exist without the liquid – then Berkeley did not regard mind as a substance in that accepted sense. For since for him minds are not like self-subsisting containers, they need something to perceive or act about, hence they need objects, the other basic existing thing in Berkeley's dualism. Berkeley makes this clear early on in the PCs, where in 478, he writes: 'if there were no sensible ideas there could be no soul, no perception ... '; and in 547, he asserts that 'we must have ideas or else we cannot think.'

Probably the main mistake underlying the monist interpretation is the assumption that substance dualism is the only form of dualism. So as my teacher, A. A. Luce, the great Berkeley scholar of the twentieth century, rightly insisted, the relation between mind and object for Berkeley is not one of substance and modes, as in most metaphysical systems, but is a perceptual or epistemic one. That allows the mind and its ideas to be mutually dependent on each other, yet still be two 'entirely distinct' things, as Berkeley puts it in PHK, section 2. So as Berkeley later explains in

PHK, section 49, and its counterpart in the DHP, ideas are not modes of the mind in the way that yellow is a mode of gold. They don't inhere in it, since for him qualities are in the mind only as they are perceived by it, that is, not by 'way of *mode* or *attribute*, but only by way of *idea*' (section 49). Hence minds and ideas are interdependent. But minds do have primacy over ideas or objects, in that for Berkeley we human beings are minds, rather than objects or ideas.

This, then, is why it is wrong to consider Berkeley a monistic idealist, or the vice versa of a monistic materialist, like Hobbes, who holds that everything is a mode of the one reality, that is, matter in motion, even consciousness and conscious ideas.

Section 6
The phenomenalist interpretation

In the previous section, I examined the monistic (mis) interpretation of Berkeley's philosophy, according to which Berkeley believes that everything that exists is mental or psychical, so either a mind or a mode of mind. This, I argued, is a serious misunderstanding of what Berkeley actually held. However, there is another monistic interpretation of him which is even more serious. For one thing, whereas the former is made by many nameless interpreters, this one is made by a number of notable philosophers from the eighteenth to the twentieth centuries, including Thomas Reid, Arthur Schopenhauer, George Grote, J. S. Mill and A. J. Ayer. According to this interpretation, the logic of Berkeley's philosophy is such that there is and can be only one kind of thing, which has been described by a variety of names, one important one being phenomena. This, too, is a monistic interpretation. Hence according to Ayer, for example, Berkeley's philosophy should, when rightly and most valuably understood, be seen as phenomenalism, that everything that exists is phenomena.

Now while I think it as important to contest all monist interpretations of Berkeley, I think it is probably more important to challenge this one rather than the previous one. For this one concerns not just the interpretation of Berkeley's philosophy, but also its truth. For if the phenomenalist interpretation is true, then Berkeley's dualistic philosophy is false and so history – a museum piece, a significant museum piece, but still only a stage in the development of truth. I think that is a mistake.

The phenomenalist interpretation of Berkeley has been stated in various ways, one popular way is to say that Berkeley was strong-minded with respect to matter, but weak-minded with respect to mind or spirit, which, it is suggested, stemmed from his religious background, shown in his being a bishop. So phenomenalists think that Berkeley should have rejected not only material substances but also spiritual substances, and so recognized that all we know, and all that exists, are phenomena.

To be sure, most phenomenalists recognized that Berkeley himself believed in dualism, but they point out that the logic of his philosophy should have made him see the truth of phenomenalism. And one key thing supporting this phenomenalist interpretation, as against his dualism, is what Berkeley says in PHK, section 27. The key sentence of section 27 is: 'Such is the nature of *spirit* or that which acts, that it cannot be of it self perceived, but only by the effects which it produces.' But if we cannot directly experience mind, even our own mind, but know it only by an inference from its effects, then how can we be sure that mind or spirit does exist? So at the least, we cannot be as certain that we exist as a mind as we can of the objects perceived. But it is worse than that, since phenomenalists would argue that what Berkeley says against material substances can be used against Berkeley's belief in spiritual substances. Hence consistent empiricism should not only begin with objects, but also end with objects, because they are the only things experienced.

So, in effect, phenomenalists agree with those who think that Berkeley is not a dualist, as discussed in the previous section – but for totally opposite reasons. For phenomenalists, Berkeley is not a dualist because there are no minds, only objects or phenomena. Whereas according to the other monistic interpretation of Berkeley, he is not a dualist, because really there are only minds and their mental objects.

Section 7
Overview

Having, in section 3 above, introduced the crucial subject of how Berkeley thinks we know our minds, I now propose to give a clear overview of my (and Neo-Berkeley's) position on this subject, and then fill in certain important details in the following sections.

While Berkeley's dualism is clearly stated in PHK, section 2, what is not clear is why Berkeley believes it to be true, that is, his justification for it. Thus it might seem that he is justifying it in his account of mental imaging in section 28, where he writes:

I find I can excite ideas in my mind at pleasure, and vary and shift the scene as oft as I think fit. It is no more than willing, and straightway this or that idea arises in my fancy: and by the same power it is obliterated, and makes way for another. This making and unmaking of ideas does very properly denominate the mind active. Thus much is certain, and grounded on experience …

Berkeley does seem to be saying here that we know our active mind by experiencing it in image creation, according to which the mind wills an image (say of the Statue of Liberty) and 'straightaway' the image arises in the mind. So images come into being by our willing them. But what is not clear is whether the willing is purely active or whether it is, to some extent, a passive object, so a volition. And this uncertainty is already present, as we have seen, in the ambiguity in PHK section 1 about operations of the mind, which could be either acts or objects. And if the latter, then, like sensory objects and memories, volitions would be passive. But then our willing images would not provide evidence and justification for the active mental side of dualism. And this seems in line with what Berkeley's states in the previous section 27, that the mind is not directly aware of itself, but only knows itself indirectly by its effects. That, as we shall see, goes with his notional understanding of self. To be sure, Berkeley did seem to think that while image creation does not give us pure and direct experience of the active mind, that it was good enough for us to feel justified in believing we have such a pure active mind. But Neo-Berkeley is more rigorous here. He thinks that 'good enough' is not really good enough when it comes to such a crucial matter. Moreover, he thinks that Berkeley provides an entirely satisfactory account and justification for the pure, active mind in *De Motu*, sections 30 and 40. For here Berkeley seems to be asserting, as against what he says in PHK section 27, that we can be directly and immediately aware of our active minds in our willing. This is what Neo-Berkeley and I call the core dualistic experience, or cde, which is very close to what Leibnitz calls apperception, according to which the mind can, at least on some occasions, not only perceive objects but can also simultaneously perceive itself perceiving objects. However, according to what I shall call the section 27 doctrine, this is not possible, because the only things we directly or immediately perceive are passive objects or perceptions. According to the section 27 doctrine, which goes with notional account of mind, we have no direct or immediate experience of our actively causing or willing anything.

As Neo-Berkeley and I understand Berkeley, he comes closest in the PHK to holding that we are purely active, and are directly aware that we are, in image creation, so in section 28. Yet he realizes that it is only the best we can do, which he thinks should be good enough. So, according to Berkeley, I believe I willed an image, by observing that an image appears 'straightaway' following my willing it. But that is not the same as directly and simultaneously experiencing my willing as the cause. Rather I infer that I am the cause, which Berkeley thought was good enough because the gap between my willing and the effect was so tiny that it could be ignored. But for Neo-B and Hume that tiny gap makes all the difference. For Hume and other phenomenalists and monists, it means that there is no justification for dualism. Hence dualism is defeated. But for Neo-B, this is not the case, since it is justified by the cde, where there is willing and awareness of willing at one time. I think this is also what Leibnitz had in mind when he speaks of apperception. So Neo-B thinks that Leibnitz is right here, but Neo-B thinks Leibnitz is wrong to believe that all human beings can apperceive. So in this, Neo-B accepts what Hume and other phenomenalists say about themselves, that they have no apperceptive experience or no core dualistic experience i.e. cde. This is crucial, but it is bound to seem both strange and outlandish. Hence a good deal more needs to be said about it by way of elaboration. But putting it very simply and directly, according to Neo-B there are two kinds of human beings: monists, like Hume, and dualists, like Berkeley. This is what Neo-B calls the Dualist Monist Typology, or DMT, about which more is said below and in part two.[3]

Section 8
Hume's phenomenalism

What is phenomenalism? One neat definition is given by Geoffrey Warnock in his *Berkeley* 1953 (p. 236), which is that it is 'Berkeley without God'. And this shows what for many philosophers and historians of philosophy is the way philosophy moved from Berkeley to Hume. But though Warnock's definition is neat and helpful, it leaves out the most important element which phenomenalism also denies, namely the human mind or self as a pure active perceiver distinct from objects and perceptions. And here it seems an appropriate place to quote Hume's famous denial of minds or selves, which is in his *Treatise of Human Nature*, 1739, Book one, Part iv, section vi, where he also summarizes his phenomenalistic position:

> For my part [Hume writes], when I enter most intimately into what I call *myself*, I always stumble on some particular perception or other, of heat or cold, light or shade, love or hatred, pain or pleasure.

I never can catch *myself* at any time without a perception, and never can observe anything but a perception …. If any one on serious and unprejudiced reflection, thinks he has a different notion of *himself*, I must confess I can reason no longer with him. All I can allow him is, that he may be in the right as well as I, and that we are essentially different in this particular. He may, perhaps, perceive something simple and continued, which he calls *himself*; though I am certain there is no such principle in me. But setting aside some metaphysicians of this kind, I may venture to affirm of the rest of mankind, that they are nothing but a bundle or collection of different perceptions, which succeed each other with an incredible rapidity, and are in perpetual flux and movement.

From this, we can now see why the issue under discussion is so crucial. For if the section 27 doctrine is Berkeley's considered view, then Berkeley himself could be the first phenomenalist opponent of dualism, even before Hume, although without realizing it. All that is required are a few adjustments, which Hume provides. The first and most important is that since we have no experience of our minds as perceivers distinct from the objects perceived or willed, then there is no reason to believe that such active minds exist. So really all that exists are objects or phenomena. Hence according to many philosophers and historians of philosophy, when Berkeley's philosophy is rightly, that is, logically understood, it is seen to issue into the monism of phenomenalism, first clearly formulated by Hume.

But we and Neo-B think these historians are wrong to write off Berkeley's dualistic philosophy in that way, so see it as a stepping stone to Hume and phenomenalism. Our reason is that the section 27 doctrine is mistaken, for we dualists do experience our mind and its acts directly and immediately in the core dualistic experience, or cde.

However, here Neo-Berkeley makes one simple but crucial qualification, briefly mentioned above, but important enough to be repeated, that is, that this is not true of all human beings, for he accepts that Hume and other phenomenalists did not or do not have the cde or apperception. Hence Leibnitz was mistaken in thinking that apperception was something had by all human beings. From this it follows that there are two basic types of human beings: monists and dualists.

There can be little doubt that Berkeley would have found this idea of two basic types of human beings outlandish, at least initially. And this might well be the response of many readers of this work. For this reason we think it is best to leave this topic for the present, until it is taken up again in fuller detail below and also in part two.

Now I want to focus on how, according to actual Berkeley, we do know our minds. Here we could begin by considering what he says in either the PHK 1710 or the DHP 1713. However, it is probably best to look first at the DHP, where Berkeley has Hylas (who speaks for the materialist) object to Philonous (who speaks for Berkeley) in a way that suggests the phenomenalist view of mind. Thus Hylas says: '… if you can conceive the mind of God without having an idea of it, why may not I be allowed to conceive the existence of matter, notwithstanding that I have no idea of it?'

One reason why this encounter is important is that in Berkeley's answer through Philonous to Hylas's challenge, we can be said to see the first published statement of Berkeley's notional understanding mind; the only notable thing that is missing is that he doesn't describe it as notional or use the term 'notion'. Here I quote what is most essential in Philonous's response to

Hylas. It contains the following five sentences, which I number accordingly:

… [1] I own [says Philonous] I have properly no idea, either of God or any other spirit; for these being active, cannot be represented by things perfectly inert, as our ideas are. [2] I do nevertheless know, that I who am a spirit or thinking substance, exist as certainly, as I know my ideas exist. [3] Farther, I know what I mean [note: 'mean' not experience] by the terms I and myself; and I know this immediately, or intuitively, though I do not perceive it as I perceive a triangle, a colour, or a sound. [4] The mind, spirit or soul … is plainly it self no idea, nor like an idea. [5] Ideas are things inactive, and perceived: and spirits a sort of beings altogether different from them.

It is in the second and third sentences that we find the notional account of self, which is bolstered by what Philonous says in the first and last sentences, which is basically the section 27 doctrine. What is also important about what Philonous says is that now that we know what the notional understanding of mind or self is, we should also be able to see that it is already, that is, implicitly, present in the PHK, first in section 2, but also in sections 139–140. For I think that what sections 2 and 139–140 (which refers back to section 27) are saying is the same as what Philonous says, only putting it in other words, that is, that the terms I or myself do not stand for any ideas, but yet I know they are meaningful. So in this way I know immediately or intuitively that I am an active being different from my ideas.

Moreover, in the 1734 revision of the PHK, Berkeley went one step further and made the helpful addition to section 140 of: 'or rather a notion of spirit'. But this only gave formal expression to the notional doctrine which was already there in all but name in 1710. My conclusion then is that once we understand what Berkeley is saying in what I quoted above from the DHP, we can see that it is already very much in the PHK 1710, although somewhat more clearly expressed in the DHP because all the important elements are together in one place.

Section 9
The cde

Now I want to bring in what we do NOT find in any clear way in the PHK 1710 or the DHP 1713. This is the core dualistic experience, or cde. Hence it seems that Berkeley did not see any need to bring it in either in 1710 or 1713. But this is not the case in the next philosophical work he published, namely *De Motu*, 1721. For in *De Motu* his account of the self and his justification for dualism are very much about the cde. Here is what Berkeley says in *De Motu*:

> 21. There are two highest genera of things, body and soul. A thing extended, solid, mobile, having a shape and endowed with the other qualities which present themselves to the senses we have knowledge of with the help of the senses, but a thing that has feeling, perception, intelligence we know by some inner consciousness. [Note that some translators,

including Luce, render the Latin 'conscientia quadam interna cognovimus' as 'a certain internal consciousness'.]

30. There is given an active res cogitans [thinking substance] which we experience [NB] to be a principle of motion in us. This we call soul, mind, spirit; there is given also a res extensa [extended substance] inert, impenetrable, mobile, which differs toto caelo [totally] from the former and constitutes a new genus.

31. From what has been said it is clear that those who assert active force, action, a principle of motion to be truly present in bodies, are embracing an opinion not founded on any experience, … By contrast those who wish mind to be the principle of motion are putting forward a view backed by their own experience [NB] and approved by the votes of the most learned men in every age.

40. In truth, by the help of the senses we perceive nothing other than effects or sensible qualities, and corporeal things which are totally passive, whether they are in motion or at rest. Reason and experience persuade us that there is nothing active beyond mind or soul.

My conclusion is that with these quotations, we have a very different understanding of mind or self, and how it is known, so a solid justification for dualism very different from the notional and section 27 account in the PHK 1710 and DHP 1713. In the DHP 1713, Berkeley emphasizes that we KNOW or UNDERSTAND our minds in an unmediated way, so immediately, but not in the way we perceive objects, which is as ideas. And yet, he says, that while we have no idea of our minds or ourselves, we know what we mean by these terms, and so know that we exist as minds. This is the notional understanding. However, in *De Motu*, sections 30 and 40, Berkeley says that we do EXPERIENCE our minds, and in section 21, he speaks of knowing our minds by some 'inner consciousness' – all of which I take to be another way of expressing the cde. So the *De Motu* understanding of self and justification for dualism are different from the notional as present in the PHK 1710 and DHP 1713. And the *De Motu* account also seems to contradict the section 27 doctrine. For according to *De Motu*, we CAN experience our own minds, which he denies in PHK section 27. The cde is also different from the notional account of self in that, unlike the notional, it seems to have two distinguishable elements, in the way that the head of a snake can be distinguished from its tail; so the cde might be compared to the way that the head of the snake can curl around and be aware of its tail.

Hence the notional and the cde are both ways that Berkeley's dualism might be understood and justified, and they also look quite similar. For it is not so easy to see the difference. Thus both agree that the knowing must be distinguished from the perceiving of objects, as set out in PHK, section 1. But I think the notional, taken together with the section 27 doctrine, sees the difference as clear and total. Hence I think the dualism it justifies can be helpfully described as pure dualism. Whereas with the cde, while it also distinguishes itself from the perception of objects or ideas, the difference is not total, which comes out in my image above of the snake. So I think we can situate the cde somewhere between perceptual knowing and notional knowing. Hence we can say that, while the cde is not as pure as the notional, neither is it as clearly empirical as the perceptual experience of objects. The truth is: the cde is messier. But then why hold it in preference to the purer notional? For two decisive reasons. The first and most important is that it IS the experience of dualists, including Berkeley, although he plays it down in preference to the notional. So the cde was the experience of Descartes, Leibnitz, William Hamilton, John McTaggart, G. E. Moore, among others. And it is also my experience as well as the experience of many living persons, especially philosophers, who I have questioned in one-to-one discussions over more than ten years. But many of those I questioned were also confident that they did not have the cde, so – like Hume, Bradley, James, Ryle and Ayer – they were monists.

Moore comes close to characterizing the dualist's experience in the way I do above in his 1921 review of Russell's *Analysis of Mind* in the *Times Literary Supplement*, namely that it is empirical but not as clearly empirical as the perceiving of objects. And in his 'Refutation of Idealism', 1903, he also observes that it is very hard to describe the dualistic experience clearly or precisely. Thus he says that no philosopher has so far done so, and he doubts whether even he has done so. However, what I believe Moore did not realize was the source of the difficulty, which is that half the human population do not have the experience, because half ARE monists, so the truth of Dualist Monist Typology or DMT.

……… ……

Here I want to make an additional point before going on to consider Berkeley's account of the self and dualism in works after *De Motu*. This concerns Hume and the big picture. My question is: how would Hume have regarded Berkeley's notional and the cde accounts? I think he would have regarded both as mistaken, but for different reasons. He would have regarded the cde as metaphysical fantasy, for in his famous statement I quoted above, Hume is clear that he has no experience of the cde and believes that no one actually has. On the other hand, I think he would have been puzzled by Berkeley's notional account in that he would not understand how it could justify dualism. What Hume might have thought is that all it can justify is the sane, common sense of self, which neither he, nor anyone else, denies. But that, he would add, is beside the point, since that is not philosophy, only sane common sense, so not a threat to his phenomenalism and monism. And Neo-Berkeley and I agree with Hume on this. But we differ with Hume on the cde, for we believe that we do have it, and that it provides the needed justification for dualism. But that does not mean that dualism defeats monism. For according to Neo-B and the DMT both monism and dualism are true, since there are two basic types of humans, the dualists and monists.

Section 10

Alciphron, the TVV and DHP 1734

After *De Motu*, Berkeley issued *Alciphron* in 1732 and the *Theory of Vision Vindicated*, TVV, in 1733. In *Alciphron*, dialogue IV, section 4, Berkeley seems to be restating his section 27 doctrine that the only way minds can be known to exist is by their effects. The discussion here is about the existence of God and is between Euphranor, who stands for Berkeley, and Alciphron, a materialistic freethinker, who accepts the science of his day. In the course of the dialogue, Euphranor sets out what Berkeley later describes as 'a new and unanswerable proof of the existence and immediate operation of God' (see his TVV, section 1). The key issue is, again, how we know minds, which Berkeley introduces by a discussion of what were called animal spirits. These are what we would now call neuronic connections and which Alciphron (in IV.4) describes as 'the messengers ... running to and fro in the nerves' which allow for "communication" between the mind and outward objects'. Alciphron accepts that these animal spirits exist, and since he had just asserted his general commitment to empiricism, that all our knowledge is derived from sense experience, Euphranor is then able to ask him: 'By what sense do you perceive them?' To which Alciphron responds: 'I do not perceive them immediately by any of my senses. I am nevertheless persuaded of their existence, because I can collect it from their effects and operations.'

This looks like the section 27 doctrine. However, by a soul, Alciphron does not, as he says, 'admit an immaterial substance', for the soul might be just very subtle parts 'residing in the brain'. The important point is that the soul or animal spirits are not the 'object of sense itself, but inferred from appearances which are perceived by sense'.

Following on this line of questioning, Euphranor then asks Alciphron whether 'I cannot, therefore, know that you, for instance, are a distinct thinking individual, or a living real man, by surer or other signs than those from which it can be inferred that you have a soul?' To which Alciphron agrees.

So what we have here seems in line with what Berkeley says in section 27, but the problem is knowing how far Berkeley himself accepted it. For one thing, it is Alciphron, not Euphranor, who brings up and affirms the existence of animal spirits and how we know them. So Berkeley's apparent agreement with Alciphron on this matter might be strategic or ad hominem. And that this is a real option is shown in the fact that if animal spirits are physical, which is what Alciphron seems to be saying, then Berkeley would not accept that they can be active causes at all; for as physical they can only be objects perceived and hence passive.

However, as the dialogue continues, it moves from animal spirits to the mind, whatever that is, whether material or immaterial; and here Euphranor does seem to be speaking for Berkeley and speaking as Berkeley does in section 27. Yet note again that Euphranor never asserts anything or even agrees with Alciphron; he only asks certain questions, and it is Alciphron who agrees and so assents to certain theses, most importantly that the mind cannot be directly known but only known by its effects. And there is an additional problem. When Berkeley says that we can only know minds by their effects, is he including himself, as 1st person perceiver, or is he only speaking of other minds? One piece of evidence which indicates the latter comes in the next section where Euphranor concludes the first stage of Berkeley's argument for God's existence with the following speech: 'Will it not then follow that this vastly great or infinite power and wisdom [which produces the physical world] must be supposed in one and the same agent, spirit, or mind; and that we have at least as clear, full, and immediate certainty of the being of this infinitely wise and powerful spirit, as of any one human soul whatsoever *besides our own*? [my italics.]' The qualification at the end is surely important, but it is not clear if it indicates that Berkeley is stating that he, as perceiving mind, experiences himself directly, which would be the cde, or whether he is holding that he knows himself as directly as he can, by a rapid inference from effects, and so as an object, which would be what he says in PHK section 28, as glossed by his section 27 doctrine and notional account of mind.

Berkeley's next work after *Alciphron* was the TVV, 1733. The two sections of the TVV which are relevant to the above question are 11 and 12. Here is what Berkeley says:

11 The objects of sense, being things immediately perceived, are otherwise called ideas. The cause of these ideas, or the power producing them, is not

the object of sense, not being it self perceived, but only inferred by reason from its effects, to wit, those objects or ideas which are perceived by sense. From our ideas of sense the inference of reason is good to a power, cause, agent. But we may not therefore infer that our ideas are like unto this Power, Cause, or active Being. On the contrary, it seems evident that an idea can be only like another idea, and that in our ideas or immediate objects of sense, there is nothing of power, causality, or agency included.

12 Hence it follows that the power or cause of ideas is not an object of sense, but of reason.

Berkeley says here that ideas have no power or agency in themselves, either to cause each other or themselves, so the power which has produced them cannot be found in them, but can be 'inferred by reason' from them as effects. And that does seem very close to his section 27 doctrine. Berkeley also says that we are entitled to make the inference to a power because these ideas must have some cause, since everything has a cause – which was accepted as self-evident before Hume. But it is not clear that he is here excluding that we can know the power by the cde. What he is ruling out is that we can experience the power in perceiving ideas, that is, sense data. But that is accepted by Neo-B.

Nor need Neo-B deny that inference can help us to understand ourselves as an active power. So it seems that what Berkeley says in the TVV does not help us to settle the question of his attitude to the cde.

Although after the TVV, Berkeley issued the *Analyst* and the *Defense*, which are important contributions in the philosophy of science and mathematics, they do not bear on dualism and so they, too, do not help us to settle our question. But his next publication does. This is the 1734 edition of the PHK and DHP, where Berkeley made a number of additions, in which, I believe, he states both the notional and the cde accounts of mind. Thus the cde comes in PHK section 89, where he adds that we have 'inward feeling' of our minds. And in the DHP he says that we 'know or are conscious of our existence'. Both 'inward feeling' and being 'conscious of our existence' are very close to the cde as asserted in *De Motu* and so go against the section 27 doctrine.

But if he accepted the cde in 1734, then why did he not delete the section 27 doctrine from section 27 in the 1734 edition of the PHK? My answer, to put it bluntly in a word, is that Berkeley was self-deceived, which I shall shortly elaborate on. But to put it very briefly, he did not want to give up a number of advantages of the section 27 doctrine, which he would have to give up if he was clear about the implications of the cde. Moreover, Berkeley did not think he needed to give up these advantages since he had his notional account, which he thought did by itself justify his dualism, and in a way that does not contradict the section 27 doctrine, as the cde does. Yet he did add the following sentence to section 27 in the PHK, 1734, which summarizes his notional account, and which might even be seen as qualifying somewhat his section 27 doctrine: 'Though it must be owned at the same time, that we have some notion of soul, spirit, and the operations of the mind, such as willing, loving, hating, in as much as we know or understand the meaning of those words.' So now in 1734 in section 27, although we don't have the cde, we do have something, a notion, which Berkeley seems to think is sufficient justification for his dualism. But in the addition he made to section 89, he does go further and says that we inwardly feel our minds, which is surely experiential, so essentially the cde account which contradicts the section 27 doctrine. How, then, can this apparent conflict be explained? One answer, to paraphrase the song about Tipperary, is that it is a long way from section 27 to section 89. More soberly, our conclusion is that while Berkeley did have cde, and that it did play a role in Berkeley's thinking about mind and justification for dualism, it had only a minor role compared to the notional, which was his official conscious justification for dualism. Hence he was able to ignore or put the cde to one side – when that was required.

But, then, am I saying that Berkeley was being disingenuous? No, rather, as mentioned above, I think it was more a matter of self-deception mixed with unclarity on what is a subtle matter. So I want to say that all along Berkeley knew, but not in a clear way, that he was directly conscious of his mind or mental acts, for I believe he did have the cde, and that made him confident that his dualism was true. But having the cde, he should have, in our Neo-B view, fully accepted the cde and abandoned the section 27 doctrine and the need for the notional account. Instead of that, we find that he keeps the section 27 doctrine, and puts the notional account of self at the forefront, which does not contradict the section 27 doctrine. It is in this way that he is able to hold onto the 2 or 3 advantages, which I discuss below in section 8. So I think that Berkeley, the otherwise clear thinker, was not clear in his thinking about the nature of mind and the dangers of the section 27 doctrine. For if he was thinking clearly he would have seen that the section 27 doctrine undermined his dualism, and that it could not be rescued by his notional account, that only the cde could do that. For though it is evident to us, because it has been pointed out by so many philosophers and historians, Berkeley did not see that his arguments against matter could be applied to his account of mind – which is what Hume is generally taken to have done in his *Treatise*. So it seems that though Berkeley was an acute and far-sighted philosopher, he could not really imagine someone like Hume coming forward and rejecting mind in the way that he, Berkeley, had rejected matter. And yet, it will be objected, how can that be right given what Hylas says to Philonous, which I quoted above, and even more in the long section he added to DHP in 1734 – which I shall now consider, which is virtually an essay on our topic. However, I quote only the second encounter, where Hylas says to Philonous:

> HYLAS. Notwithstanding all you have said, to me it seems, that according to your own way of thinking, and in consequence of your own

principles, it should follow that you are only a system of floating ideas, without any substance to support them. Words are not to be used without a meaning. And as there is no more meaning in spiritual substance than in material substance, the one is to be exploded as well as the other.

PHILONOUS. How often must I repeat, that I know or am conscious of my own being, and that I myself am not my ideas, but somewhat else, a thinking active principle that perceives, knows, wills and operates about ideas. I know that I, one and the same self, perceive both colours and sounds: that a colour cannot perceive a sound, nor a sound a colour: that I am therefore one individual principle, distinct from colour and sound; and, for the same reason, from all other sensible things and inert ideas. But I am not in like manner conscious either of the existence or essence of matter. On the contrary, I know that nothing inconsistent can exist, and that the existence of matter implies an inconsistency. Farther, I know what I mean, when I affirm that there is a spiritual substance or support of ideas, that is, that a spirit knows and perceives ideas. But I do not know what is meant,

> when it is said, that an unperceiving substance has inherent in it and supports either ideas or the archetypes of ideas. There is therefore upon the whole no parity of case between spirit and matter.
> HYLAS. I own my self satisfied in this point ...

What is so striking about Hylas's second challenge is that it seems so close to what Hume actually says in the *Treatise*. It is also striking that Berkeley's first reply to Hylas's first challenge seems to be the cde, that is, that he is 'conscious' of himself. But it is worth noting that Berkeley weakens this somewhat by adding 'or knows', which is more in accord with the notional account, which Philonous then develops more fully. Philonous's reply to Hylas's first challenge is less important than his reply to Hylas's second, although his statement in his first reply, that 'the being of my self, that is, my own soul, mind or thinking principle, I evidently know by reflexion', is interesting. But since Berkeley does not elaborate on what he means by 'reflexion', there is no way of knowing if he means the cde or the notional or a bit of both.

So my conclusion concerning this long addition to the DHP 1734 is that Berkeley, as well as Hylas, was 'satisfied' that there was no serious danger to his basic dualism from a Humean direction. So I think that Berkeley's mixture of a bit of cde and a lot notional, blocked him from clearly seeing the real danger of Humean phenomenalism. But again, how could Berkeley, the otherwise clear thinker, not see this? And my answer, again, is that he didn't see it because he didn't want to see it because of the two or three advantages he got from the section 27 doctrine and his notional account.

… … ….

After the 1734 edition of the PHK and DHP, there is one other philosophical work which Berkeley issued, namely, *Siris*, 1744, his last, which I discuss in detail below. But, to anticipate, Berkeley nowhere mentions in *Siris* the Humean danger, although Hume's *Treatise* had been published five years previously. Nor does Berkeley clearly bring in the cde in the way he does in *De Motu* and in the two statements he added to the PHK and DHP in 1734. Instead, notions are very much to the fore, although the cde could – as I shall suggest below – be in the background.

Then finally there is his 1752 edition of *Alciphron*, where he makes the following addition to VII.5: 'Certainly it must be allowed that we have some notion that we understand, or know what is meant by, the terms *myself, will, memory, love, hate*, and so forth; although, to speak exactly, these words do not suggest so many distinct ideas.' What this shows, I think, is that notions had clearly won the day for Berkeley; since there is no indication in any changes in 1752 that Berkeley was thinking more positively about the cde, so nothing about inward feeling or consciousness of self, or any kind of direct experience of mental acts.

Section 11
James Hill on the notional

I think the commentator who has gotten closest to Berkeley on notions is James Hill. According to Hill, Berkeley holds that we know our minds or selves immediately, intuitively and transparently, in our mental acts – but not BY our mental acts, since that, I take it, would go against the immediacy of the notional understanding of self. So the notional is very pure and immediate and transparent, which justifies my description of it as pure dualism as against the messiness of the cde. Thus there is no division in the notional understanding of mind, as there is in my snake image, as mentioned above (section 9). It is a pure intellectual knowing or transparent intuition. That makes it sound strange and arcane; but really, according to Hill, our notional understanding of ourselves is most evident and familiar to all of us. For all of us know, unquestionably, that we are selves that exist. And indeed, I think Hill's position is that the very familiarity and evidence of the notional have probably stood in the way of its being correctly understood.

Now, as mentioned above, I think that it was this notional account of mind which Berkeley thought justified his dualism. But as I have also tried to show, (1) he also goes some way towards accepting the cde in *De Motu* and his cde additions in 1734, and that, according to Neo-B and I, while the cde can deal with the threat from Hume's phenomenalism and monism, the notional is unable to do so. Only the cde can do that. However, that is not Hill's view. He thinks the notional can deal with the Humean threat, and that his account of the notional is not only true as an interpretation of what Berkeley held, but that it is also true as such.

Now probably one thing which makes this subject so difficult is that both accounts, the notional and cde, agree that we do not experience ourselves as an idea or object, so in the way I experience my computer screen. And Hill, as I understand him, is also critical of the section 27 doctrine, for he thinks that the notional is immediate and transparent, so does not require the mediation or inference of ideas as effects. So a reader might well ask: What, then, is it that distinguishes the two? And my answer is that the cde is experienced, whereas I do not think the notional is. More specifically, because the cde is experienced, it occurs in time. It has a beginning and end, whereas I do not think this can be said of the notional. Rather, it seems to be always there. And this is crucial for actual Berkeley's account of immortality, and also for its role in his so-called master argument, as I explain in the next section.

Section 12

The 2 or 3 advantages of section 27 doctrine

I have stated above that Berkeley was unwilling to give up the section 27 doctrine, according to which we can have no direct or immediate experience of our mind, because of the advantages that it gave him. Now I want to describe these advantages. One advantage is that it bolstered his account of the immortality of the soul in supporting the claim that the mind or soul was completely different from the objects we experience in the world, hence not subject to what everything in the world is subject to, namely, coming to an end. But if we know our mind directly by the cde, then we know it by experience and in time. Then our awareness of it is occurrent. But if it is occurrent then it can come to an end. And in fact, as a dualist, I know that my cde does frequently end, but also begins again, in short, that it is intermittent.

The notional, however, as I understand it, is not experienced, so not occurrent or in time, as is the cde.

With the cde, while I experience myself, I know I – a self different from any object or idea – exist. But when the cde ceases, then I lose that assurance about myself as an existing thing distinct from what I perceive. So when I die, it could be the case that I shall not be having the cde. Hence the cde does not provide grounds for a belief in immortality such as Berkeley gives in PHK, section 141.

Here it might be helpful if I explain what I mean by comparing what I have just said to Descartes's account of the cogito and his understanding of himself as a thinking being. That is, in the second *Meditation*, Descartes makes the point that he can be sure that he is a thinking thing, but only while he is thinking. And that is my understanding of the cde. But Descartes himself goes further later in the *Meditations*, where he argues that he and we are essentially thinking beings, and so that we are always thinking, even when asleep, although we don't always remember that we are always dreaming or having some form of mentation. Hence we can be confident that our dualistic self always exists, and will exist when our bodies die. Now while Berkeley's notional account doesn't move in this Cartesian way, Berkeley does hold that there is no reason to believe that our selves are not always present, hence they will not come to an end and cease to exist when our bodies die. Hence his notional understanding of self is far more supportive of a belief in immortality than that of the cde.

To make this clearer, here is what Berkeley says in PHK section 141:

> We have shown [Berkeley writes] that the soul is indivisible, incorporeal, unextended, and it is consequently incorruptible. Nothing can be plainer, than that the motions, changes, decays, and dissolutions which we hourly see befall natural bodies (and which is what we mean by the *course of nature*) cannot possibly affect an active, simple, uncompounded substance: such a being therefore is indissoluble by the force of nature, that is to say, *the soul of man is naturally immortal.*

Indivisibility and simplicity are clearly crucial. And they are not a feature of objects we perceive in the world, whereas they do seem to be in accord with Berkeley's notional theory account of our selves. And we are also aware of them in the cde. But the problem is that the cde is intermittent. It is also only fair to point out that the cde does seem to have two elements and be somewhat composite which comes out in my snake image, and also in the cde itself, where I am aware and aware that I am aware. But it also needs to be mentioned that I experience these simultaneously. But still, as I pointed out above, the cde is more empirical and so less pure, simple and indivisible than the notional. James Hill puts this nicely, when he says that with the notional 'we know ourselves through ourselves'. So with the notional there is pure oneness, which fits with Berkeley's argument for immortality, which is not the case with the cde.

And in addition to this theological advantage, there is an arguably even more important advantage to Berkeley in respect to his immaterialism in accepting the notional rather than the cde. For crucial to Berkeley's critique of matter is that what we perceive are only passive, mind-dependent objects or ideas. But if I can experience my self directly in inward feeling, and be inwardly conscious of my self, as in the cde, then that shows that there is another kind of experience, apart from perception of objects. And that threatens Berkeley's argument against matter. For the materialist can suggest that he experiences matter in something like that way.

I now want to consider what I think is a third apparent advantage of the notional which is also connected with immaterialism. Here we need to recall that there is a positive side to immaterialism, where instead of denying the existence of matter, there is the claim that mind is always present when there is experience of objects. Putting this somewhat differently, according to this positive side of immaterialism – which might be more accurately described as idealism – when there are perceptions, there must be a perceiver perceiving them. Now where this comes out most clearly and importantly for Berkeley is in his so-called master argument, developed in PHK, sections 22–23 and also in the DHP. Here I want to focus on it as presented in the latter, the DHP. This is where Berkeley, through Philonous, challenges his opponent, Hylas, to think of an object that is not being conceived by a mind.

To this challenge, Hylas confidently responds that he is now conceiving a tree in the forest where there is no person or mind nearby able to perceive it. But against this, Philonous replies that Hylas does not realize that he, as conceiver, must be conceiving it. And Hylas accepts what Philonous says. But the question is: Was Hylas conceiving this just a few moments before Philonous called it to his attention? Prima facie, he was not, since he thought he had an example of an object not conceived by any mind. But

Hylas doesn't realize this. Instead in his review of how he came to realize that he had not refuted Philonous, he says:

> ... let me consider what led me into it.–It is a pleasant mistake enough. As I was thinking of a tree in a solitary place, where no one was present to see it, I thought that was to conceive a tree as existing unperceived or unthought of, not considering that I myself conceived it *all the while* [my italics].

But was he conceiving it 'all the while'? That is exactly what Hylas should not have conceded. That he, or his mind, is conceiving it following Philonous's reply, he can and should accept, for that was his experience, which was evoked by Philonous's reply to his original assertion. But Hylas thought his experience a few moments before was of a tree which was not being conceived by anyone. And we think he should have stood firm on that, even though it is not easy to express in graceful English.

However, as against our suggestion, it is just here that Berkeley can bring in his notional understanding of the self, which, unlike the cde, is not limited by experience and time. For what the notional understanding of self expresses is the truth that I, as mind or person, am always present when I am thinking or perceiving, or comparing, etc. Nor need I verify this by experiencing myself to believe it. For no sane person would deny it. For it is a practical matter which goes deeper and is practically unquestionable, moreso than a philosophical theory. For it is not a philosophical theory, it is sane common sense. But it is different with the cde. That is part of a philosophical theory, justified by experience. That is, there are times when I do know that I, a mind or thinking principle, am perceiving or conceiving an object, such as a tree, and am aware of myself so doing. And, according to Neo-B, when Hylas, following Philonous's reply, became aware that he was conceiving the tree, he would have been having that experience. But that experience, the cde, is intermittent. So Hylas was having the cde at that time, but not before. Before 'his' experience was only of the tree as an object. And that is the experience that monists, like Hume, always have, since as monists they do have the cde.

So I believe the cde cannot help Berkeley in supporting his master argument and idealism, or dealing with the monist rejection of it. And that, I believe, is why the notional was so important to him. It seemed to provide the support that is required to sustain his idealism and immaterialism, dramatically expressed in his master argument. But it doesn't, for a monist, like Hume, always has the counter experience Hylas had prior to Philonous's reply to his initial claim. Hence Berkeley fails to show that there are no things or objects which exist without being perceived or conceived by a mind.

Section 13

What underpins the notional

Here I would like to expand on what I believe actually underpins Berkeley's notional account of self, and makes it seem to be a truth of philosophy. There are two main things: one negative and one positive. The negative is the difficulty of speaking felicitously in a phenomenalistic way about one's self. Thus Hume says that all he experiences are perceptions, hence he is just a bundle of perceptions. But then a critic of Hume can say that to know this, he, Hume, must be experiencing when he finds, as he says, no dualistic self. But if he is experiencing, there must be an experiencer, so he must be something more than perceptions. But, as Hume and his follower, A. J. Ayer, have pointed out, but Ayer even more clearly, the force of this argument can only work if we agree to designate what we are perceiving as perceptions which require a perceiver. Then, from that linguistic or grammatical or classificatory decision, the critic's argument works. But Hume and Ayer do not accept that linguistic decision, for they did not think that such a linguistic requirement should rule in philosophy. And given Berkeley's empiricism and what he says especially at the end of the Introduction to the PHK, about the way we are deceived by language, Berkeley should be the last one to base or enforce his philosophy on the conventions of language. But that, sadly, was what he seems to be doing or relying on in the notional understanding of self and the way it seems to justify his master argument, although probably without clearly realizing it.

Now I come to what I think is the positive underpinning of the notional understanding of self, which, as mentioned above, is that it draws on what I have called the sane common-sense understanding of self, which all sane, common-sense people do and must accept. For of course I accept that I am a person, called David Berman, who certainly exists. For all of us need to believe that we are a person answering to our name. Hence it is not surprising that the first thing a child is generally taught is his or her name, which they should answer to. All sane people accept this, and this includes all philosophers. But what I think is not generally appreciated is that it is more complicated in the case of philosophers than say mathematicians, statesmen, doctors, etc., because the common sense understanding of self looks like a philosophical theory. But really, I believe, it isn't. Really it isn't philosophy but sane, practical common sense. For it must be assumed in order to do philosophy. So it should be put to one side and not come into philosophical discussions.

Have I given a satisfactory account here of what underpins the notional account of self? I would like to think so, but I doubt it. Yet I hope that I have gone some way towards doing this.

Section 14
The big historical picture

In section 10, above, I suggested that because Berkeley was anxious to retain the two or three advantages of the section 27 doctrine and notional account of mind, he was unable to imagine how the actual Hume could appear and threaten to undermine his philosophy. But the actual Hume did appear, who, it is widely believed, brought about the defeat of Berkeley's dualistic philosophy. Thomas Reid was probably the first to clearly describe this, which, with additions by Schopenhauer and others, has become the canonical way of telling the story of early modern philosophy from Descartes to Kant and beyond.

This begins with the claim that the only thing we can directly perceive are ideas, which is what Descartes introduced and Locke developed further – which is sometimes called the 'new way by ideas'. From that it follows that we cannot directly perceive or experience anything which is not an idea, which principle Berkeley uses to reject matter, but which

Hume then goes on to use to reject minds and spiritual substances. So, according to this simple but widely accepted canonical story, Hume's phenomenalism undermines minds, just as Berkeley's immaterialism undermined material things.

Here I might observe that there is good evidence that this canonical story was around before Reid. Thus some years ago, I discovered a letter from Francis Hutcheson, written from Dublin, to William Mace of Gresham College, in which Hutcheson writes: 'I was well apprized of … your notion of our mind as only a system of perceptions, I imagine you'll find that *everyone* [my italics] has an immediate simple perception of *self* … As to material *substrata*, I own I am a sceptic … '. This letter, which was written in 1727 but only published (posthumously) in the *European Magazine* in 1788, shows that there was at least one phenomenalist before Hume and that, while Hutcheson was not one of them, he seemed to understand Mace in a phenomenalist way. Unfortunately, we do not have Mace's reply to Hutcheson, but we can imagine that he might have and should have responded that not everyone does have an immediate simple perception of self, since he, Mace, does not have it. So he was a Humean monist before Hume, whereas Hutcheson was a dualist, like Berkeley, even being skeptical of material substance.

Another piece of evidence that the canonical story was around before Reid is to be found in the first memoir of Berkeley, which was written by Oliver Goldsmith and published in 1759. This is the story that Goldsmith tells about how, when Berkeley was walking one day in College Park in Trinity College, and absorbed in thought, he hit his head against a post, and a waggish student looking on said: 'No matter, Dr Berkeley, never mind.'[4] But this was not a joking matter.

In his 1762 *Enquiry*, Reid develops the canonical story more soberly and expansively and with a touch of drama. He begins by praising Berkeley and Hume as probably the two most acute philosophers of the time. Yet, though Berkeley, Reid says 'was no friend to skepticism, but had that warm concern for religious and moral principles which became his order ... [Berkeley held] the serious conviction, that there is no such thing as a material world; nothing in nature but spirits and ideas ... '. Reid then observes that 'Berkeley's arguments are founded upon the principles which were formerly laid down by Descartes, Malebranche, and Locke, and which have been very generally received.'

The main principle is that what we immediately and directly experience are only ideas or sensory objects. Reid then points out that Hume 'proceeds upon the same principles [as Berkeley], but carries them to their full length; and as the Bishop undid the whole material world, this author, upon the same grounds, undoes the world of spirits, and leaves nothing in nature but ideas and impressions, without any subject on which they may be impressed.' In short, Berkeley believed that 'by giving up the material world, which he thought might be spared without loss, and even with advantage, he hoped, by an impregnable partition, to secure the world of spirits. But, alas! [laments Reid, Hume's] *Treatise of Human Nature* wantonly sapped the foundation of this partition, and drowned all in one universal deluge.'

To Reid's story, we might then add that according to Schopenhauer, the foundations which were sapped by Hume were restored – at least to a great extent – by his hero, Kant. Then Schopenhauer adds that he (Schopenhauer) builds on but goes further than Kant because he discovered what Kant had thought was unknowable, namely the thing in itself, which according to Schopenhauer is Will to Life. Of course, there have been many alternatives to how the story should be continued after Kant, but what is generally agreed, what is canonical, is that it starts with Descartes, then moves through Locke to Berkeley, then to Hume, then to the great compromiser, Kant, woken from his dogmatic slumbers by Hume, who brings together the (positive) Continental rationalist tendencies with the (negative) British empiricist tendencies, in his great Transcendental compromise which gives due regard to both, so should be accepted by everyone. But Neo-B and I think the story goes wrong, because Hume's monism does not defeat Berkeley's dualistic philosophy as it can be justified by the cde.

… … …

I have been focusing on the active self side of Berkeley's dualism and his complex understanding of it in his various works. But Berkeley also had interesting things to say about the other side of his dualism, the object side, which is the subject of the next section.

Section 15

Berkeley on objects:
The revision

In PHK section 1, Berkeley describes the ways that objects come to be known. It is by means of the sense impressions from our five senses:

> By sight I have the ideas of light and colours with their several degrees and variations. By touch I perceive, for example, hard and soft, heat and cold, motion and resistance, and of all these more and less either as to quantity or degree. Smelling furnishes me with odours; the palate with tastes, and hearing conveys sounds to the mind in all their variety of tone and composition.

Prima facie, this seems an entirely acceptable account, until we learn that for Berkeley these sense impressions do not, in fact, enable us to perceive physical objects, if by physical objects we understand objects existing independent of the mind. For as Berkeley says in section 3, the being of physical things consists in being perceived. So slowly and by gentle steps Berkeley introduces his radical theory, that there are no physical things independent of our sense impressions or perceptions. This is his immaterialism, which we have already said a good deal about above. And one thing that needs to be mentioned again is that for him objects can be understood in two ways: as the familiar medium-sized objects, like apples and tables, or the sensory elements they are composed of. And it is the elements that Berkeley is primarily interested in. But, of course, the elements he has in mind are not material elements, not material atoms or corpuscles, but sensory or perceptual atoms, which, he maintains, are what we immediately or directly experience. They are the perceptual or epistemic equivalent of the atoms or corpuscles which the science of the time regarded as what apples and all material things are composed of. So instead of the world being composed of material atoms, Berkeley thinks the world is composed of what we immediately and directly experience by the five senses, the smallest of which are sensory atoms.

This, in short, was Berkeley's original theory in the PHK, which is also to be found, although not so succinctly stated, in his DHP, and, with respect to vision and touch, in his NTV. But there is strong evidence that, starting with his TVV of 1733, Berkeley came to see that his original theory needed to be revised, for he came to see that there were problems with the putative sensory atoms. This revision then appears even more dramatically in his *Siris*, 1744, when his dualism becomes more Platonic, so where, in line with Plato's Allegory of the Cave, physical objects become shadowy, flowing, fluxy objects.

How then did Berkeley come to see difficulties in his original account as presented in the PHK? I take it that it was when, in preparation for Part 2 of the PHK, he tried through introspection to perceive the sensory atoms of the five senses, and found that it was much more difficult than he originally thought.

And this led him to see that the force behind the mixing or uniting of these putative simple sensory elements into medium size, common-sense objects, such as apples, was extremely difficult to overcome, even if there are such elementary sensory objects. For behind this force, Berkeley came to realize, was God Himself. Berkeley expresses this in the following way in the key thirty-sixth section of the TVV with respect to visual experience.

In the contrivance of vision, as that of other things, the wisdom of Providence seems to have consulted the operation rather than the theory of man; to the former things are admirably fitted, but, by that very means, the latter is often perplexed. For, as useful as these immediate suggestions and constant connexions are to direct our actions; so is our distinguishing between things confounded, and as it were blended together, no less necessary to speculation and knowledge of truth.

And yet the later Berkeley still believed that it was worthwhile moving in the direction of the elementary and unblended. How? By the kind of introspective or psychological analysis, which is brilliantly but briefly summarized in PHK, section 1, but which, I suggest, Berkeley found it more difficult to carry through in a detailed way. In short, it was hard by introspective psychological analysis to get to the sensory atoms of the five senses. And probably he had the time to try to carry out this work when he was in Rhode Island, 1729–31, with little else to do but wait for the promised money to come through for his Bermuda project. However, while Berkeley came to see that it was God who had confounded our theoretical understanding by blending our sensory experiences, he also recognized that God has been generous and good to us in this blending and mixing activity – but good in a practical way that parents are good to their young children in trying to prevent them from knowing or coming into contact with harmful substances and powerful realities, such as erotic pleasures, which parents do by telling their children stories they know to be untrue. But just as parents hope that their children will eventually grow up and be able to understand reproduction and experience erotic pleasures, so, Berkeley suggests, God did not intend that everyone should be kept forever in a childish, mistaken (yet useful) epistemic state, in believing there are bodies, which are both seen and touched, which can exist independently of minds in external space, that is, the belief in realism and materialism.[5]

And this was also the view of Schopenhauer – the first great philosopher to recognize the importance of what he took to be Berkeley's idealism – who said that to become an idealist was to grow up, to be enlightened and that Berkeley had made the most important step in bringing us to this grown-up condition. But for Schopenhauer, this development had nothing to do with God, since like other Berkeleian atheists of the time, he saw the spiritual part of Berkeley's philosophy as deeply mistaken. But for Berkeley, it was most important.

In short, I suggest that Berkeley came to see himself as carrying out God's will in bringing those mentally mature enough to idealism, in short, from the childish exoteric belief in realism and materialism to the grown-up esoteric belief in immaterialism and idealism. Nor is it surprising that Berkeley would see this, since he himself was an esotericist in his own life and philosophical work. Indeed, in section 35 of the TVV, just before the section I quoted above, I think Berkeley is alluding to his esoteric strategy in his NTV, of 'admitting divers things as true, which in a rigorous sense are not such, but only received by the vulgar and admitted for such'. But though this is acceptable initially, that is, for the vulgar, Berkeley then points out that

> The work of science and speculation is to unravel our prejudices and mistakes, untwisting the closest connexions, distinguishing things that are different, instead of confused and perplexed, giving us distinct views, gradually correcting our judgment, and reducing it to a philosophical exactness [hence esoteric truth]. And, as this is the work of time, and done in degrees, it is extremely difficult, if not impossible to escape the snares of popular

language, and the being betrayed thereby to say things strictly speaking neither true nor consistent … For, language being accommodated to the praenotions of men and the use of life, it is difficult to express therein the precise truth of things, which is so distant from their use, and so contrary to our praenotions.

So in this way, Berkeley connects his own esoteric practice in the NTV with that of God, as set out in section 36. But even in section 35 itself Berkeley can be seen as making this connection, since not only is Berkeley forced to use (popular) language to express his truths, but so is God in what Berkeley calls God's visual or optic language, which makes us wrongly believe that what we see is what we touch and vice versa. (On God's visual language, see *Alciphron*, 1732, dialogue 4.) So by 'untwisting connections', especially the 'long and close connection in our minds between the ideas of sight and touch', which makes us think of them 'as one thing', Berkeley thought that he was indeed bringing about a profound enlightenment of mankind – at least for those mature enough for it – from the childish realist state in which God had, perforce, hitherto put humanity. For like his own practice, this enlightenment works 'by degrees' and through time, in stages. But now, with Berkeley's philosophy, human development has entered a crucial stage. If Berkeley recognized this, which I believe he did, then it must have filled him with an awesome sense of his mission.

Now as a matter of historical fact, Berkeley's idealism only became a major influence in the late eighteenth century, after being taken up by Kant, although in a revised, compromising way, in his *Critique of Pure Reason* (1781), but then endorsed in a more robust way by Schopenhauer, as well as others, such as J. S. Mill in a phenomenalistic way later in the nineteenth century. And it was in the nineteenth century that idealism came more and more into its own as the consensus in philosophy. Although at the beginning of the twentieth century idealism was to be hit by a number of powerful criticisms, one of which was Moore's 'Refutation of Idealism', 1903. And this was followed by James's 1904 essay, 'Does consciousness exist?', which did much to bring materialism back in fashion, after its century of being dominated by idealism, making the twentieth century the great age of materialism, as the nineteenth century had been of Idealism. (What the twenty-first century will be still remains to be seen, but at present it continues to be materialistic.)

Now I want to come back to and continue my account of Berkeley's philosophical development. For while the TVV, sections 35–38, show him questioning the feasibility of getting to simple or essential sensory elements, that did not stop him from believing in the other kind of simple essential things, that is, selves or spirits. Indeed, I suggest that, if anything, his doubts about getting to sensory atoms made him even surer about spiritual atoms, which becomes most clear in *Siris*, Berkeley's last philosophical work. For here Berkeley is clear that the object world does not have the cognitive stability he previously thought it had, that it is flowing and in flux – in a way similar to how, in the Allegory of the Cave, Plato describes physical things as shifting, unstable shadows. That in *Siris* Berkeley is distinguishing his present view from his earlier view is crystal clear from what he says in *Siris*, section 347:

> Upon mature reflexion the person or mind of all created beings seemeth alone indivisible, and to partake most of unity. But sensible things are rather considered as one than truly so, they being in a perpetual flux or succession, ever differing and various.

So while Berkeley came to disbelieve, or at least have serious doubts about sensory atoms, he also came to believe even more in minds or persons or souls as spiritual atoms, as the only beings able to partake of unity. So while the later Berkeley lost something he had in his early philosophy, he also gained something. For while the early Berkeley did, of course, believe in minds or spirits, the later Berkeley believed in them even more, that is, that only minds or spirits truly existed in a fixed elemental and essential way, as unitary beings, and that only minds can be truly known (*Siris*, sections 297, 305).

To be sure, Berkeley did, earlier on, believe that he knew that minds are unitary and indivisible, and hence immortal; but the way he knew it was through a conceptual argument, which he summarizes in PHK section 141. Now, in *Siris*, he appears to know this more directly by intuition or experience. Although he also uses reason to some extent, as well as his close reading of the history of philosophy, especially Greek philosophy and especially Plato.

Section 16
Berkeley's *Siris*

Having described in the previous section how Berkeley revised his account of objects in the TVV and *Siris*, I now want to look at *Siris* on its own. However, straightaway I should say that it is not easy to see what Berkeley's overall philosophical position is in *Siris*, because it is so different from his works of 1709–1713, which are paradigms of analytic clarity and consecutive reasoning. Hence it is not surprising to find Berkeley himself describing *Siris*, in section 297, as 'this rude essay'. And yet he is reported to have said that *Siris* cost him more trouble than any of his earlier works. Given all of this, it is also not surprising that philosophers, and even Berkeley scholars, have not paid the same attention to *Siris* that they pay to his works of 1709–1713.

And another problem is that in *Siris* Berkeley usually presents his views largely in the context of the history of ancient Greek philosophy, and especially the philosophy of Plato, who is Berkeley's hero in *Siris*.

But then readers can easily be misled by Berkeley's avowed Platonic sympathies into thinking that his position in *Siris* must have brought him away from his earlier empiricism. I think this is wrong, for I think that *Siris* is as empiricist, that is, experiential, as his earlier 1709–1713 works. And it is also wrong, because I think Plato himself is more an empiricist, that is, experiential, than is generally recognized.

However, apart from these factors, which have discouraged most philosophers, and even commentators, from taking *Siris* seriously, there is one factor which cannot be laid fully at Berkeley's door, which is that commentators have failed to see that *Siris* should not be read in the normal consecutive way, starting with page one, then to page 2 and so on to the end. Why not? Because it is just not that kind of consecutive work, as Berkeley himself says in section 350. It is more suggestive, more concerned to give hints rather than prove or argue for anything.

Connected with this is that by the time present-day readers get to the philosophical part of *Siris*, which is in the last third of the work, most readers are jaded by reading what has come before – so like having eaten a big meal, just before being served a subtle gourmet dish. So they are tired out by reading about tar-water, about (old) medical practice, chemistry, etc, in the first two-thirds of the work.

The gourmet dish begins with section 290, but it is anticipated in section 109, then 253, 263–265, which might be seen as a preface and introduction; or, we might say, an appetizer. One reason for seeing section 290 as the philosophical beginning of *Siris* is that it is so much like the first two sections of Berkeley's PHK.

What Berkeley says in section 290 is then developed in the next seven sections, up to 297, where Berkeley speaks of 'The mind, her acts and faculties, [which] furnish a new and distinct class of objects'. But, according to Berkeley, very few people can get into this class, since the great majority of people are immersed in the other extreme, that is, of what is grossly sensible. For getting to the 'purely intelligible' is an attainment which involves 'tedious work' and 'struggle' (section 296).

This then, I believe, is the right way to read *Siris*, so starting with section 109, then going to sections 253, 263–265, and then moving quickly to the key sections 290–297, which need to be read carefully; then reading to the end of the work – although leaving out or only skimming some otherwise interesting sections.

Section 350 is important as indicating the purpose of *Siris*, according to Berkeley, and how it differs from his early work. What he is proposing here, he says, are not 'principles', as in the PHK, whose title I take it he is alluding to. Thus he is not trying to prove anything, but only offering 'hints' to 'awaken' and 'exercise' the mind, so that it might experience rather than understand. What this suggests, I think, is that in *Siris* Berkeley is advocating something like meditation, as in the Eastern tradition, but differing from it in being dualistic rather monistic.

In section 297, Berkeley divides human beings into two groups, those (the great majority) who are immersed in matter, in physical appetites and sensory experience and a small minority who have come to know themselves as essentially minds, rather than as just living, physical beings – a division which is anticipated in section 263 by Berkeley's broad division of ancient philosophers. So this select group have come to know, according to Berkeley, that there is 'another order of being, the mind and its acts' (section 293), and that minds are the only true unitary beings, unlike all the physical objects, which only seem to be unitary beings. But this is known, not by means of a logical argument, as it is or was in PHK, section 141, but by experience gained in the struggle and ascent into the clear light of real things.

I suggest that this new way of doing philosophy goes with his formulaic revision in section 290, which revises his dualistic position as set out in PHK section 2. For now it is not that mind and its objects are 'entirely distinct' but that 'Body is opposite to spirit or mind.' Now they are contraries, which makes it more feasible to see humans as two opposed types, the bodily and the mental, differing in degree or ratio, as in Plato's account of the three types in the *Republic*. However, these are not types as understood by Neo-Berkeley, as in the DMT, since for Berkeley all humans are dualistic in nature and should be aiming at being purely mental, even though none can be as purely mental as God, who is, as Berkeley says in section 290, the only pure mind or spirit. According to Neo-Berkeley, however, human beings are essentially either dualists or monists, and should aim to realize their true deep nature as one or the other.

Although the sections of *Siris* that are most philosophically relevant begin most importantly with 290, I begin with section 109, which is on time, and where Berkeley offers a practical suggestion about achieving the highest good. This is close to the suggestion that he made to Percival in a letter of 1709 about becoming one's own friend, which, I think, shows the unity of Berkeley's thinking. But probably a more important indication of its unity is that the theory of time adverted to in *Siris*, section 109, is the radical theory Berkeley develops in PHK section 98. And this could be important, since there is a good deal of evidence from Berkeley's PCs that he saw his theory of time as providing an independent argument for the immortality of the mind. In short, according to Berkeley, the flow of our ideas is not just the way we measure time, as it is for Locke and Descartes, but constitutes time; hence there can be no time when (and in which) we do not exist. (See Berman 1994, chapter 3.)

What Berkeley says in section 290 is crucial. But it is also complicated. Thus while it is primarily about the spiritual versus the bodily, it also concerns sensory types – which I hold is the next most important typology after that of monist-dualist, which is examined in detail in part two, section 7.

In *Siris*, section 292, Berkeley speaks of the real world as the 'order of beings, mind and acts', but that in this world a human being is constituted by 'contraries', and that there is a 'struggle in his nature between ... flesh and spirit ... during which conflict the character fluctuates' between the two. In section 295, Berkeley's focus is on the ascent 'from the sensible into the intellectual world … [where] the mind contains all, and acts all …'; and similarly in 296, where he describes 'the struggle upwards into the light of truth', and in 297, where 'The mind, her acts and faculties furnish a new and distinct class of objects' different from her normal self and former objects and previous prejudices. Here, importantly, I think he is describing his own meditative experience, his struggle to realize his spiritual character – or, as Neo-Berkeley would say, to BE a dualist, and not just to know that dualism is true.

In sections 333 and 334, Berkeley describes the ways that Socrates and Proclus, the Neo-Platonist, think we can get to the true self and even further. For in contemplating God we know ourselves. And it is the self or person, of all created things, that Berkeley believes has real unity and so truly exists. Whereas in his early work, as we have seen, Berkeley thought that elementary sense-data also had unity and essence; but now he thinks they are in flux or flowing.

Therefore, attaining the most perfect experience of our self is crucial, according to Berkeley, as I understand him, for it enables us to get into the realm of Forms, where each of us is, like the Forms, also one and unchanging and truly exists. (Compare Plato's *Phaedo*, 76–82.) Indeed, the Forms exist absolutely, whereas our selves are less perfect, because, living in the world, we are always tempted or distracted by sensory objects and bodily desires. So even the most advanced persons lose their best experience of themselves. As Berkeley puts it in section 337, even the 'most refined human intellect, exerted to its utmost reach, can only get imperfect glimpses of the divine ideas', 'the most real' things. For as Berkeley says in section 340, the mind can mount, ascend, get a 'glimpse', but then it drops down again. So we might say that for Berkeley we human beings are amphibious, for though we live almost entirely in this material world, we are able to live briefly, at moments, in the other, higher intelligible world. But we should, as Berkeley says in 341, struggle to get and stay in the 'upper region' as far as we can.

Putting this more generally, I think that in sections 337–347 Berkeley is adverting to his own experience of getting out of the Cave and catching a glimpse of the Forms, and also of God, since, according to Berkeley, God is largely constituted by the Forms – of Wisdom, Goodness, Justice, etc. So I think when he is describing Plato's position in the *Phaedrus* (in sections 366 and 367), he is also implicitly describing his own position and experience, which might therefore be described as either Platonic Berkeleianism or Berkeleian Platonism.

I have gone into some detail in describing the philosophical part of *Siris* because I believe it is important, especially given Berkeley's suggestion in the last section of *Siris*, section 368, that he has now seen 'fit to weigh and revise' his 'first fruits', that is, his philosophical views in his early works of 1709–1713.

But that is not my only reason for trying to understand what Berkeley is getting at in *Siris*. For arguably the most important reason is that it enforces the Platonic view that we, or some of us, can actually come to know THE truth, so know things in themselves, and cease groping about in the shadowy darkness of the Cave. And it seems to me that Berkeley is offering practical hints on how this can be done.

… … … …..

Now, at the close of part one, I want to come back briefly to the question of the notional versus the cde account of mind, and consider whether there is anything in *Siris* which is relevant to the interpretation I gave above. The first thing to say is that there is much in *Siris* which could be relevant, but, unfortunately, nothing that is clear-cut and decisive. Thus there is no statement in *Siris* of the cde that is as clear as those in *De Motu*, where Berkeley says that we know ourselves 'by some inner consciousness' (section 30), or as clear as the 1734 addition he made to PHK section 89, that we have 'inward feeling' of ourselves. However, in *Siris* section 291, Berkeley does say that we are 'conscious' of initiating motions in bodies, which he suggests we know by experience. And this is in accordance with *De Motu*, section 21, where he says that we experience our thinking substance to be a principle of motion in us. (And I should probably also note that what Berkeley says in *De Motu* and *Siris* was not an innovation, since as early as the PCs, entry 648, he states: 'We move our legs ourselves. tis we that will their movement.') However, Neo-B thinks that what Berkeley says seems questionable because moving our bodies is much too like activity in the physical object world. So willing our hand to move should not be seen as its efficient cause but the occasion for certain hand-moving sense data to appear, which is the way Berkeley explains causality in the world of inanimate objects. It is also interesting that in *Siris*, Berkeley does not bring in image creation which in PHK section 28, he seemed to think was what gave us the best experience of activity, and ourselves as active (dualistic) beings. One explanation for this is that on account of his now being a much older man, Berkeley ceased being a strong imager. (See A. C. Fraser's 1891 essay.)

However, probably the most interesting thing that Berkeley says in *Siris*, which could be evidence of the cde, is his description of the ascent into the intelligible realm, and the inevitable falling back into the bodily and appetitive condition, which, he says, happens again and again. For here Berkeley could well be describing his having the cde and the losing it; for the cde, unlike the notional awareness of self, is occurrent and intermittent. The problem is that Berkeley does not say enough to justify interpreting what he says about ascent and descent as clear evidence that he is referring to the cde. But, on balance, I am inclined to believe it probably does refer to the cde, since I believe he had the cde, but was reluctant (consciously or unconsciously) to bring it to fore, for fear of losing the two or three advantages. I also think it is worth noting that there is nothing in *Siris* which suggests that he repudiated the cde. However, what he actually says is all about notions, which term he uses again and again.

… … …..

PART TWO

NEO-BERKELEY

Section 1
Berkeley in 1752–1753

In order to get a clear idea of actual Berkeley's final philosophy and how it is to be distinguished from that of Neo-Berkeley, let's imagine speaking to Berkeley in 1752–1753, sometime after he had settled in Oxford and finished preparing his *Miscellany* and new edition of *Alciphron* for publication. Now at the end of his philosophical and literary career, he would be able to reflect on its full output of nearly fifty years, with all its developments and modifications.

Suppose we first asked him: Are you a dualist? That is, do you believe that there are two kinds of beings, active minds and passive objects, and that you are one of the former and not the latter, so know yourself to be a mind that perceives and acts about objects? We feel totally confident that he would answer Yes, which fits what we have been saying throughout part one.

Suppose we then asked him: Do you believe that the existence of objects depends on their being perceived by minds, which are distinct from them?

Here I think he would also answer Yes. But this, Neo-Berkeley believes, is a mistake, because Hume and other phenomenalists do experience themselves as only objects or perceptions existing without being perceived by a mind or thinking principle distinct from them. And while Berkeley might initially try to hold on to his idealism, we believe that he might be persuaded to give it up, that we could convince him that he was mistaken.

But even if he could not make that move, Neo-Berkeley would then ask him a more limited question. This is: where does your greater certainty lie, in idealism, or in the core dualism? Here I believe that though Berkeley might not like the question, he would have to say that he was more certain of the latter, hence agreeing again with our position throughout this work, that it is dualism that is essential to his philosophy.

Why would he have to say this? I think because his idealism is dependent on the truth of the core dualism, since the dualism sets out the basic elements, that is, minds and objects, and relation between these elements which are then used to establish a further truth – which, I think, is how Berkeley himself proceeds in PHK sections 1–3.

Probably one reason why this is not so apparent is that for Berkeley the core dualism, as he understood it, was so evident to him that he probably felt that little needed to be said in support of it. Whereas while he thought that idealism was also true and possibly even evident, I think he realized that more analytic and argumentative work was needed to show its truth. For, as he observes in section 4 of PHK, there is an 'opinion strangely prevailing amongst men, that … sensible objects' can exist without a mind perceiving them. And so what he proceeds to do in much of the PHK is to oppose this strangely prevailing opinion, whereas he felt that no one could seriously doubt that he or she was a mind or self different from the objects he or she perceives; for Berkeley probably thought that anyone who could doubt this could hardly be brought to accept his idealism.

Therefore the logic of Berkeley's actual philosophy begins with the core dualism, then moves to idealism and then to God. Neo-Berkeley holds on to the core dualism, and develops it, but sheds Berkeley's idealism and understanding of God and in their place adds one main thing: the DMT, the two basic types, the dualistic and monistic, both as true and not just in theory but in life.

Because the core dualism seems so evident to a dualist, especially a strong one, like Berkeley, it is hard for a dualist to consider that it might not be true of all human beings. And there is a universalizing assumption which runs not only throughout Berkeley's writings but all philosophers, which, more specifically, can be seen in the two other great British empiricists, Locke and Hume. This is clear even from the titles of their principal works:

LOCKE: *An Essay concerning human understanding*, 1690

BERKELEY: *Principles of human knowledge*, 1710

HUME: *A Treatise of human nature*, 1739–1740

HUME: *An Enquiry concerning human understanding*, 1748

So the assumption is that there is one generic element, which underlies the way all we humans experience and understand, so there is one HUMAN nature and understanding. But Neo-Berkeley thinks this is deeply mistaken, and is what he calls the Typical Mind Fallacy, or TMF. For he holds that being human is not basic or elemental. Rather what underlies it are two things: dualism and monism. So being human is like the colour green, which is a mixture of the primary colours, yellow and blue. Or it is like the water we see and drink, which is composed of hydrogen and oxygen.

Hume, the third great British empiricist, is probably most explicit that human nature is basic, uniform and universal; although, to his credit, he does consider it possible that it is not so, that there are fundamental differences between humans, differences which are philosophically relevant. This comes out, as mentioned above, in his memorable passage on the self, which I quoted in part one, section 8 where he says that if someone claims to experience a distinct self, different from objects, then 'All I can allow him is, that he may be in the right as well as I, and that we are essentially different in this particular … '. Hume also goes into the possibility that human nature is not the same or uniform in his 1748 *Enquiry*, section viii, 'On liberty and necessity', which he begins by considering why the dispute between determinists and free-willers has been going on for so long and is still not resolved. Here again he adverts to the possibility that it might be explained if 'the faculties of the mind' were not 'naturally alike in every individual'. But that he says is 'impossible', for if it were true, then 'nothing could be more fruitless than to reason or dispute together'. So, as he observes a few paragraphs later: 'Mankind are so much the same, in all times and places … [and there are] constant and universal principles of human nature … '. The explanation that Hume gives for the continuance of the dispute is the ambiguity of key terms. And I think Hume is right that the disputants are using language ambiguously, but that, I would argue, can be traced to their different basic experiences; so it is similar to two people speaking at cross purposes, which goes deeper than their ambiguous use of their language.

However, once the assumption of one basic human nature and understanding is called into question, and the typical human mind is recognized as a fallacy, then a new possibility is introduced: that there are two basic types, the dualist and monist, hence the Dualist Monist Typology, or DMT, which explains the different and conflicting views of philosophers. Of course, there must be some thing or things which human nature is and which all humans have. To begin, there is our common physical identity, shown especially in our ability to procreate with each other. There is also our capacity to operate in huge communities with other humans. But most important, we believe, is our linguistic ability, which unites us and enables us to work together in a concerted way. These three make up our sociolinguistic nature, which more than anything else makes us humans and persons, and distinguishes us from other animals.

... ...

Section 2

The DMT: Why it hasn't been accepted

But how, it will be asked, can dualism and monism both be true? For it seems to be contradictory. Neo-B's reply is that they are not contradictory opposites but contraries; and that each type knows what its nature is by direct experience, a dualist by the cde, whereas a monist, like Hume, by being aware that all his experience is of perceptions without any perceiver distinct from these perceptions.

Another way of explaining why the the DMT is not contradictory is by considering the sense of hearing and its deficiency in those who are deaf. For here, too, it can be asserted that humans have and do not have hearing, which could be a contradiction. But that is only so if the two conditions, of hearing and being deaf, are universalized. But there is little danger of the deaf universalizing their condition, or of those with hearing not recognizing that there are some human beings with a hearing deficit. But, then, why has this not been recognized in the case of monists who have the cde deficit? I think the main reason is because it does not affect a person's normal functioning. Hence it is not as easily observed as by those who are deaf. The deficit in sight is the hardest to deny, then comes hearing, then smelling and then tasting. Touch stands on its own for reasons that we go into below, in the last section below. After the deficit of tasting, and close to the deficit of the cde, is that of mental imaging, which was first identified by Francis Galton, in the 1880s, who drew on the deficit of colour blindness which was only identified in the late eighteenth century by John Dalton. So the deficits that are hardest to identify are those that have the least noticeable effects on normal functioning or behaviour.

Section 3

Berkeley's immaterialism and monotheistic God

As Berkeley himself took the liberty of treating his philosophy as living and so open to change and revision – for example, on the nature of sensory objects in the TVV, 1733- so Neo-Berkeley thinks he should be allowed the same liberty. For after all, as Berkeley insists in *Siris* section 368, our primary allegiance should be to the truth and not loyalty to a philosopher or a philosophy at a given time. (As Aristotle is supposed to have said: 'I love Plato, but the truth more'; so Neo-Berkeley would say: 'I revere actual Berkeley, but the truth more.') And I think that if Berkeley were able to learn of Neo-Berkeley's views, he might be interested, although no doubt he would initially be shocked especially by Neo-Berkeley's rejection of his monotheistic God.

Why Neo-Berkeley speaks of the monotheistic God is that he does not reject all gods, for he holds open the possibility that there are beings superior to human beings. So while he is an atheist in respect to the monotheistic God of Judaism, Christianty and Islam, he is not a total atheist. And he also accepts Spinoza's God or Nature, that is Spinoza's pantheism, so the monistic counterpart of the dualist's plurality of finite gods.

While it is important to understand Berkeley's actual philosophy as he understood it – which is the proper work of the scholar, and which we have tried to do in part one – we do not think that scholarship is enough, if a philosophy is to be living force and not just a museum piece. And this again is in line with what Berkeley says in section 368 of *Siris*, which can be considered his philosophical memoir and testament, that truth should be 'the chief passion' of a philosopher, who must always be prepared to 'weigh and revise'.

In short, as Berkeley revised his earlier positions, which he pursued with ardour in the early period of his life, so we think he would have been open to the possibility that his own final position in 1752 would also need revision. But now it is up to we Berkeleians, who believe that Berkeley's philosophy was essentially right or right at core, to develop his philosophy, hence to be Neo-Berkeleians, just as Berkeley himself was a Neo-Berkeleian compared with his earlier philosophical positions.

But how, it will be asked, can a philosophy that sheds Berkeley's idealism and God still be regarded as Berkeleian? My answer is: first, because it retains Berkeley's core dualism and goes further with it than Berkeley did, but also because it draws on elements or tendencies within Berkeley's philosophy, which Neo-Berkeley believes are moving in the right direction. So Berkeley's core dualism is given greater emphasis – partly because released from the baggage of his idealism and monotheistic God.

According to Neo-Berkeley, some minds are only objects or perceptions which exist without a mind distinct from them. Thus Hume and others of his type are object-minds, and hence are monists not only in theory but in experience and life. But while Neo-Berkeley agrees with what Hume says about himself and his type, he does not accept Hume's universalizing of his experience and type. For there are also dualistic minds, like Descartes, Berkeley, G. E. Moore, who are constituted of the two fundamentally different elements, minds and objects, and are perceivers distinct from the things they perceived – the perceivers having reflective awareness of themselves, at least at times, as something distinct from the objects they perceive.

Neo-Berkeley accepts that phenomenalists and other monists lack this reflective awareness, or what Neo-Berkeley calls the cde, and that it seems to involve splitting consciousness, which is thought to be impossible. But just as some of those with little or no mental imaging regarded, and still regard, mental images and mental imaging as impossible, so Neo-Berkeley and I are not dismayed by this criticism, since we are confident that we have the splitting-consciousness experience, and for us experience has primacy over alleged conceptual difficulties.

Section 4

Neo-Berkeley on God and other dualistic minds

For actual Berkeley, there are two kinds of minds: finite human minds and the infinite mind, God. And just as Neo-Berkeley calls into question Berkeley's idealism, so he also calls into question the existence of Berkeley's monotheistic God. The rejection of Berkeley's idealism and God is negative. But there is also a positive side to Neo-Berkeley's atheistic denial of God. One way of expressing this is to say that what seems to be lost in rejecting the infinite mind is actually gained in respect of finite minds, that they are recognized to be greater than believed by Christians such as Berkeley. Here it is useful to go back to the origins of Christianity to see that what Neo-Berkeley is doing is reversing what Christianity did to the then prevailing polytheistic system. For the Christians were themselves atheists in that they rejected the many finite gods and demigods of the Greeks and Romans. What the Christians did was to put in their place the one, monotheistic God of Judaism. What Neo-Berkeley is doing is reversing this, so proposing if not a return to the older polytheistic system, at least a willingness to take the older system as a serious possibility, although in a refined form. Putting it simply, he thinks that the gods have character but not personalities, so not as they appear in Homer. (On this, see below, section 6.)

But it is one thing to propose and another thing to justify, that is, provide reason and evidence for holding that one is true and the other is not. In what follows, I try to show that Christian monotheism is false or at least questionable, and what Neo-Berkeley proposes is supported by at least some evidence.

Section 5

God and theistic and dualistic intimacy

It was generally accepted by philosophers before Hume, most notably by Locke, that the existence of God could be demonstrated by means of the principle of causality, by what is usually called the cosmological argument. For Locke this argument was based on the principle that 'nothing cannot produce any real being', which for Locke is the second most evident truth, the first being that 'man has a clear perception of his own being', in short, that he exists. For Locke maintains that anyone who denies that he exists can scarcely be worth arguing with, which is what I described above as the sane common-sense belief in self. Locke then proceeds to show by means of the principle of causality that since we are aware not only of our existence but of our intelligent activity – if only in assenting or not assenting to his argument – that it follows that our intelligent activity must either have come about from itself or from God as its cause. But since it cannot have come from ourselves, since how could we create our own intelligence, it must have come from God, as He alone would have the power. Therefore, Locke concludes that a powerfully intelligent God must exist.

Now probably the most important way of seeing what is wrong with this argument is to focus on the way that it does not clearly distinguish a cause and its effects. And this applies not only to God and His activity, but also to ourselves and other minds. So if I hear you talking intelligently, am I listening to the cause of the intelligent speech or only to its effects? Prima facie or common-sensibly, it seems that I am experiencing you as the intelligent cause, and not just hearing effects. But Locke himself recognized that what I actually, that is directly or immediately, hear when I hear someone talk, are only sounds, phonemes, which I infer have been produced by an intelligent cause. But the inference is made so quickly and habitually that I am not consciously aware that I have made it. However Locke doesn't make much of this; whereas Berkeley did, especially at the end of his NTV – which I quote below in section 7 – and in the PHK, where he tightens up the idea of causality, and makes a clear division between what we immediately and directly experience as against what we only mediately experience and infer in the perceptions of objects, a distinction he insists on in *Alciphron*, Dialogue 4 and even more clearly in the TVV, as discussed above.

However, what specifically interests us now is how the distinction relates to section 27, where Berkeley says that the mind and its activity are not known directly but only by their effects. Here in his account of mind, he is taking the distinction very far – too far as we have argued at length in part one – where we argued that dualists do experience themselves directly at times in the cde. This is crucial, as true activity is essential to the cde. But Berkeley was keen on taking the distinction very far, given the uses he puts it to in his critique of matter, and his defense of immortality, also in the light-hearted opening it gave him in *Guardian* 130, where he states the section 27 doctrine and uses it to suggest that the freethinkers are just material machines.

Now let's bring in Hume, who as an acute reader of Berkeley sees the issue as Berkeley does, but, in hindsight, even more clearly. For Hume realizes that the focus of the distinction should be on one precise thing, which as usual in philosophy is unfortunately called by a number of names. Thus Hume uses the terms 'causal action', 'efficacy', 'agency', 'power', 'force' and 'necessary connection' to refer to this one thing.

(And he might have added another one, namely 'mental acts', which Moore uses to point to his dualistic experience.) Possibly Hume hoped that this use of various terms would help to make clearer what he had in mind, by pointing to it in somewhat different ways. But the multiplicity of names can also confuse and blur an issue. However, the acute Hume sees through the confusion, and sees that the crucial issue is to get to the experience or impression of true causal action that makes the idea legitimate and meaningful, if there is such an impression – or not, so meaningless if there is no such impression. For Hume sees that reasoning and talking about causal action without this experience cannot legitimize claiming that X is truly the active cause of Y, if we never directly experience X, but only its supposed effects. For just to call Y an effect cannot, however, common-sensibly or linguistically, legitimize the claim that Y must have been brought about by the causal action of X. To be sure, if Y is an effect then by definition it must have a cause. But is it an effect? Here we need to free ourselves from the power of words, definitions and conceptual schemes and the need to speak in graceful English. For that can make us assume that something is the case without the experience from which our idea, if it is legitimate, must come.

Hume understood this. For he was an acute introspective psychologist, able to block out the power of language – like Odysseus blocking his ears and not hearing the Sirens. And Hume realized that he was able to perceive Y in one perception, on its own, as just there, like a sound. So it can exist in itself. Hence it does not need a cause and need not, indeed should not, be described as an effect, but as just a sense experience or what Hume calls an impression, or what is in later philosophy called a neutral sense datum. And the same can be said of X.

What this shows, as against Locke, is that a sense experience or sense datum can arise without being caused, so can come from nothing, or just be, and then even become nothing in the next moment. But the important thing is to recognize that the sense experiences X and Y, can each exist on its own, so exist separate from or independent of each other. And given that they can exist on their own, Hume is able to say, surprisingly, in *Treatise*, IV. vi, that such sense-data, despite their apparent fleeting nature, fit the understanding of a substance, since existing on its own was the accepted understanding of substance.

Now where this analysis of causality is most important is in psychology and cosmology, in the putative acts of humans and the putative acts of God. So in the first we seem to experience intelligence exhibited in someone talking to us and in the second we also seem to experience intelligence in the apparent orderliness of the solar system. But while this seems so in both cases, Hume would say that we are mistaken in both. Why? Because in both cases we do not distinguish what we directly or immediately experience from what is suggested to us by what we experience, suggestions which arise powerfully from association of ideas. So instead of purely and directly experiencing what is there, the association of ideas tends to conflate or mix sense experiences, which makes us believe that we are perceiving the intelligent activity of minds. More specifically, it makes me believe that in listening to you speak, I am aware of you as an active, intelligent mind. But as Berkeley himself shows in *Alciphron* IV, probably drawing on Locke, what I am directly or immediately aware of is only the sounds or phonemes, which, without realizing it, I infer must be coming from your mind. So my experience of you talking, unless I engage in very careful introspection, is a conflation of two distinct things. Therefore the truth is that I do not directly experience you as an active and intelligent mind.

Moving now to cosmology and to the solar system, Christian philosophers and scientists were able to say, drawing on the analogy with human minds and the effects they seem to cause, that the cause of the apparent orderliness and intelligence of the solar system must also come from a mind, but one that is much greater and also outside the physical solar system itself. Therefore it must come from a designing mind which could not be a human mind since the solar system obviously requires far more power and intelligence to organize than we humans have. Therefore it must come from an infinitely powerful and intelligent mind, that is, God. Berkeley goes generally along with this cosmological reasoning, although for him the solar system is understood to be composed of sensory objects or ideas rather than material objects.

And the basis for this is section 27, where Berkeley argues this way, not only with respect to other minds, but even our awareness of ourselves and our own human activity. So he goes very far, which, if consistently pressed, leads to making his position vulnerable to Hume's conclusion, that we have no direct experience of any causal action whatsoever, even from our own minds and its mental activity. As I have argued above, while this should have worried

Berkeley, it didn't. For he had his notional account of mind, with its two or three advantages, to which we can now add a further advantage, that it enabled him to hold not only that we know that God exists, but that we know this with as much or even more certainty than we know of any other mind, apart perhaps from our own. So here Berkeley is, in effect, saying that if we want to be totally rigorous we must be solipsists. But if not, then we must accept not just the existence of other human minds but also God.

But this was not the conclusion that Hume drew. For Hume did not see the necessity to accept any minds distinct from objects, either one solipsistic mind or many dualistic minds or that of God. For one thing, unlike Berkeley, Hume did not believe that everything must have a cause. Nor did he have what Berkeley had, namely the cde, such as Berkeley describes in *De Motu* and in the 1734 editions of the PHK and DHP. What he did have was the notional understanding of minds and selves, but, as we have suggested above, he regarded that as just sane common sense, not philosophy. Hence for Hume, there is no distinct mental agency, no dualism, either in human experience or in our experience of the physical world as such. But if so, then we have no justification for believing in either active finite minds or the active Infinite Mind. And that is just Hume's phenomenalist and agnostic position in a nutshell: Berkeley without dualistic minds, either human or divine. And according to Neo-Berkeley, Hume is right that there is no justification for inferring a God who causes or orders the material world, as appears in the solar system. That the solar system has been orderly and is now orderly Neo-B accepts, since that is how we experience it. But what cannot be accepted is that the orderliness comes from an active cause distinct from it, namely God. What it comes from, we do not know. Nor do we even know that it will continue. This is Hume's agnosticism. So Neo-Berkeley is in agreement with Hume's agnosticism, which is very close to atheism and his phenomenalist account of the physical world. What he does not accept is Hume's claim that no humans have a direct experience of themselves as active minds distinct from the objects they perceive. For Neo-Berkeley is sure that he has the cde, and that the history of philosophy shows that many others had it, and that his discussions with living persons convince him that many of them have it as well. In short, the upshot of all this is that the monotheistic God is not either necessary or needed.

But are we, as Berkeley sympathizers, justified in looking away from God, especially considering how certain Berkeley was of God and His importance? I think we are. And yet it must be admitted that it is not easy to look away from God and, even more, to deny that He exists. Why is it so difficult? Because, putting this very directly, if a little crudely, it is not easy to kick a 2000-year-old habit. Nor, at a personal level, is it easy to free oneself of early and confident teaching. And one quick way I think I can show this is by telling the TCD-Jewish joke. I mentioned one philosophical TCD joke in part one, which we owe to Oliver Goldsmith, so this is an opportunity for me to tell the only other one I know. And who better to tell the joke than myself – a Jew from New York who has been at TCD since 1966. This is a joke I heard about twenty years ago, which, as far as I know, has never appeared in print. It is about an American College student from New York who decided to do his junior-year abroad at TCD in the early 1960s, so before it became popular. The student came from a liberal, upper middle-class NY Jewish background, Jewish but not at all religious, so what would now be called secular or cultural Judaism. After spending the first term at TCD, he returned to New York for the holiday period, and because this was before air travel between Europe and the United States had became popular, the whole family came to meet him at the airport, being naturally curious to know about his experience in Dublin and TCD. And so he told them about his experience at Trinity, including about the name TRINITY College. So he tried to explain how, according to the Christians, God is one but also three – the Father, Son and Holy Ghost. Now during this account of the Trinity, the boy's father was becoming visibly more and more agitated, until finally he broke in and said: 'Listen, son, there is something you need to know. In our family there is only ONE God, and He DOESN'T exist.'

In short, the one monotheistic God, whether He does or does not exist, is still the only God that many persons can take seriously. Hence it is blocking the feasibility of refined polytheism; which shows that it is not easy to change an attitude or mindset that has been in place for nearly 2000 years and has been inculcated in many persons from their early childhood.

However, Neo-Berkeley's aim here is not to argue in favour of polytheism, but to present the difficulties in believing in the one Judaic-Christian God, and how turning away from such a being can open up a more profound understanding of finite human minds.

To begin, it seems clear that in his rejection of Berkeley's understanding of immaterialism Neo-Berkeley has gone some way towards rejecting Berkeley's God, since he has eliminated the gap which immaterialism creates and which Berkeley believes is only fill-able by God. Against this, Neo-Berkeley believes that the gap can be filled in by Hume's phenomenalist account of the physical world but also by a more profound understanding of human minds than Berkeley allowed.

More specifically, Neo-Berkeley believes he can show that there are specific reasons for rejecting Berkeley's account of God. One reason can be taken from Berkeley's discussion of extreme heat and pain in the DHP. Here Berkeley says that extreme heat must be mind-dependent because we cannot experience it without also feeling pain. Berkeley likes that because, in line with his idealism, it shows that because extreme heat cannot be separated from pain, and since pain is mind-dependent, so extreme heat must be as well. But what is not welcome to Berkeley is the problem it poses for his account of God, who as the causer or creator of sensory experiences in human minds must also be the perceiver of them. Hence, it seems to follow that since God causes extreme heat in us, He must feel the pain that is inseparable from it. However, Berkeley cannot accept this, since he holds that God is perfect and feeling pain is an imperfection. But how then can we conceive God causing the extreme heat, without being aware of what He is causing, and so feeling the pain which goes with extreme heat? Hence the conclusion that Neo-Berkeley draws is that God does not cause the objects we perceive. What Neo-Berkeley accepts, as mentioned above, is the phenomenalist account of objects, according to which they are neutral sense objects or impressions, whose origin and causation we do not know, and so which we must be agnostic about. All we do know is that they appear in an orderly and regular way which we understand as the laws of nature. Hence, what La Place is famously said to have replied to Napoleon, when Napoleon asked him where God came into his system of the world, namely that he didn't need that hypothesis, is what we also can say, that is, that we, too, do not need Berkeley's God.

And to support this turning away from God, Neo-Berkeley also adds another difficulty which relates to Berkeley's concept of mind and hence to the cde. This difficulty is that, according to Berkeley, God not only creates and perceives objects but also creates and sustains human minds. That Berkeley accepts this is shown, for example, in his often quoted line from St Paul that 'In God we live, move and have our being' (see, e.g., PHK, sections 14 and 66), and also what he says in PHK, in sections 149 and 155, that we have 'an absolute and immediate dependence on' God. Berkeley also says in the concluding sections of the PHK that God is conscious of our thoughts. But it is not clear that this is consistent with Berkeley's basic account of minds as active perceivers of passive objects. The problem is that if God perceives our thoughts then don't we become passive objects rather than active minds? Well, probably not, since Berkeley does not say that God perceives our mental acts, and still less our mind itself, but only our thoughts or objects. Yet even that does seem to go some way to bringing into question the integrity of our minds. And the fact that Berkeley draws on Scripture in section 155 to make his point suggests that he realized he had a problem and had to consider his doctrine more as a revealed mystery than a doctrine of reason or philosophy.

But an even bigger problem concerns God's creation of human minds. To see why this is a problem, it is useful to look, by way of contrast, at what Berkeley says about God's creation of sensory objects, which, I think, is helpful and indeed ingenious. In short, because we know how our finite minds can create and perceive mental images, it seems plausible to infer, by analogy, Berkeley suggests, that God creates our strong sensory experiences in that way. That seems in accord and consistent with Berkeley's empiricist philosophy. But how finite minds could be created by another mind, even an infinite mind, is much harder to understand, given Berkeley's active mind, passive object distinction.

Of course, it is natural to think that if human minds are created, it must be God, the infinite mind, who creates them. For who or what else could do it? And similarly, since there is no matter or material space for minds to live and move in, then what else could they live or move except in God and his perception of them?

But must we accept that human minds were created by God? Why not believe, as Plato did, that human minds have always existed and hence are eternal, and not just immortal, which, after being created by God at a certain time, they are in the Christian system? And it is here that we can see, what I referred to above, how the rejection of the infinite God goes with an enhancement of finite minds. So while something is lost by rejecting Berkeley's monotheistic theology, something is gained in respect of human minds by accepting that of Neo-Berkeley's pluralistic theology. For according to it, while human minds are finite and individual, they are infinite in time, that is, they are eternal, whereas according to Christian monotheism, only God is eternal.[6]

Section 6
Dualistic intimacy

At one level, actual Berkeley's philosophical system is remarkably simple and economical in that it contains only minds and objects, each of which has only two species. So minds are either infinite (God) or finite (humans). And objects are either sensory (so physical objects) or images or memories, drawn from sensory objects. Yet while finite minds are clearly central in Berkeley's system, I think his personal interest in them was surprisingly limited. Of course, he was interested in finite minds, as being one himself; and he was also interested in finite minds in the way a teacher is interested in his students, who he wants to help. Yet, from the last section of the PHK, that is, section 156, it is clear that the other mind Berkeley was more interested in was not any human mind but God:

> For after all, [he says] what deserves the first place in our studies, is the consideration of GOD, and our duty; which to promote, as it was the main drift

and design of my labours, so shall I esteem them altogether useless and ineffectual, if by what I have said I cannot inspire my readers with a pious sense of the presence of God ....

From this, and also from what Berkeley says in sections 149 and 155, I think that Berkeley's highest desire was to be close to God, rather than to other human minds. This is in stark contrast with McTaggart (1906), who, like Berkeley was also a idealist and dualist, but unlike Berkeley, he was an atheist, who says that one of his reasons or motives for being an atheist is that he could not bear the thought that God should be closer to him than his friend or sweetheart – which could not be more at odds with what Berkeley says in the final section of the PHK, just quoted.

While Neo-Berkeley does not share McTaggart's hostile attitude to God, he does agree with McTaggart that finite minds contain more potentiality than Berkeley supposed, for according to McTaggart they are eternal, and they should replace God as our primary concern.

I suggest, too, that there is a connection between the way that Berkeley severely limited our understanding of and access to human minds in PHK section 27 and his desire to be closer to God. My suggestion is that distancing himself from other human minds – in knowing them only by their effects – went with his experience, or hope, of an intimate relationship and experience of God. Taking our cue from that, Neo-Berkeley draws on what Berkeley says, but goes in the other direction. By looking away from Berkeley's God and his desire to have a sense of His presence, Neo-Berkeley hopes to redirect that energy and interest to other human minds, where we know other human minds not by observing the similarity between their effects and the one's we cause, and so inferring that they are like the mind we know directly in the cde, we can have a similarly direct intimate experience of one, or a few, other finite minds.

Putting this in a converse way, Neo-Berkeley points out that the way that Berkeley thinks we know all other minds brings them and even ourselves (insofar as we understand ourselves as we understand others) to the level of the sane, common-sense persons. So, as against this, Neo-Berkeley thinks there is evidence that it is feasible for some minds to experience at least some other minds as we experience our own mind in the cde. So as in part one, we rejected the section 27 doctrine with respect to the dualist's experience of himself or herself, now Neo-Berkeley is also rejecting it in a practical way in respect to other minds.

To be sure, Neo-B believes that experiencing another mind directly is not something that can be easily done. But he thinks that there is no reason in principle why some individuals cannot have the same intimate experience of other minds which they have of themselves in the cde, which might then be described as dualistic intimacy.

Neo-B also points out that there is reason to believe that by this means we can go further than being eternal in the way we are at present, but be eternal in the way that gods and demigods are. For in our present condition we exist in time and are subject to continual reincarnations, which will continue until our eternal character becomes sustainable, that is, perfectly eternal. How is this to be done? According to both Plato and McTaggart, through the true loving relationship with another individual, which I think is very close to our idea of dualistic intimacy. Plato is clearest about this in the philosophical section of his Seventh Letter, where he describes the steps whereby two individuals can reach the truth, so get out of the Cave. McTaggart is clearest in his *Human Immortality and Pre-existence*, 1915. Here we give only the barest summary of their common dualistic position. However, for more detail, see Berman 2015 and 2016.[7]

But what evidence or reason, it will be asked, does Neo-Berkeley have for thinking that dualistic intimacy is feasible? What seems least difficult to imagine is how one mind could be directly aware of the thoughts of another, if by thoughts we mean mental images. Here the most promising source of evidence is from telepathy, which, open-minded psychologists consider the most credible form of parapsychological experience. And I think many people believe they have occasional telepathic experiences. After images, the next kind of direct perception of one mind by another would be of emotions, then mental acts. After that it would be one mind being in direct contact, or in rapport, with another mind itself. Is there credible evidence that this is feasible? And what sort of person are we looking for who could provide evidence of it? Apart from being honest, they would also need to be critical, intelligent and clear-headed with no vested interest. Now I think we find these unusual qualities coming together in the case of Montaigne and his account of his friendship with Etienne de la Boete. Here is what Montaigne says about his experience:

> … at our first meeting, which happened by chance at a great feast and gathering in the city, we found

ourselves so captivated, so familiar, so bound to one another, that from that time nothing was closer to either than the other ....Such a friendship has no model but itself, and can only be compared with itself ... it was some mysterious quintessence ...

Again:

No action of his could be put before me in any aspect that I should not immediately discern its motive. Our souls travelled so unitedly together ... [and] saw into the very depths of each other's heart, that not only did I know his as well as my own, but I should certainly have trusted myself more freely to him than to myself.

This, then, is my idea of dualistic intimacy, of one mind knowing another as it knows its own. But Montaigne was clear that this required exceptional qualities; for as he says, ' ... where a man commits himself from the depths of his heart, keeping nothing back, it is essential that all the springs of action be perfectly clean and reliable.' So here then we have a case of two minds in extraordinary rapport, where one mind is able to experience another individual in the way it experiences itself in the cde. And while

Montaigne does not develop this, Neo-B and I think that the relationship as described by Montaigne can form the basis not only of getting to the truth but getting off the wheel of reincarnation and so ceasing to be a personality and becoming a fully eternal and sustainable character, and so becoming a demigod, which we believe Plato did become. Neo-B and I think this is feasible, but that it needs to be distinguished from the cde understanding and justification of dualism or the DMT, as developed above. For we believe these doctrines are much more than just feasible. And, in the next section we introduce another doctrine, which we also believe is more than just feasible, which is important in providing additional evidence for some of the main claims of part one, especially the truth of phenomenalism concerning the world of objects. This is the Tactual Visual Typology.

Section 7
Tactual visual typology

#1: Review of Neo-B in part one

In part one, we have seen that while Neo-B supports
Berkeley's dualism, indeed regards it as essential to the
Berkeleian philosophy, he rejects Berkeley's notional
account and justification of it. Instead Neo-B believes
that only the cde account can justify dualism against
Hume's monistic critique.

Yet while Neo-B believes in the truth of dualism, as
justified by the cde, he also believes that not everyone
has that experience, and that Hume and many others
do not have it and are therefore monists. Hence he
believes that some human beings are dualist types and
others are monist types, and that dualism and monism
are both true. This is the Dualist Monist Typology, or
DMT, which is Neo-B's most radical doctrine, which
he recognizes is not an easy doctrine to accept or
indeed to understand. But he thinks it can be made
more understandable by showing how it fits with a

second typology which Neo-B also introduces, the most basic after that of the DMT. This is the typology of the Tactual Visual Types, or TVT, which is the subject of this section.

In what follows, this new typology is first briefly summarized, then, in line with our methodology, it is presented through four exemplary philosophers, Locke, Russell, Kant and T. K. Abbott, who are shown to be either visual or tactual types. Following this, we then try to explain why the visual and tactual types experience in the particular ways they do. We then go on to show that while Berkeley himself would certainly have been surprised by this new typology, it owes a great deal to him. Hence the new typology can be considered Neo-Berkeleian.

#2: Introduction of the TVT

The tactual types, or tt, are those who believe that the sense which brings them most convincingly into contact with external physical bodies is the sense of sight. On the other hand, the sense which they experience most intimately, and which gives them pleasure and pain, is the sense of touch, which therefore tells the tt more about his or her body than about external things. Hence the sense of sight can be described as their objective sense, whereas the sense of touch their subjective sense.

It is otherwise with the visual type, or vt. For the sense that the vt believes brings them most convincingly into contact with external physical bodies is the sense of touch, whereas the sense which they experience most intimately, and which gives them pleasure and pain, is the sense of sight. And it is this sense which tells the vt more about his or her body than about external things. Hence the sense of touch can be called their objective sense, whereas the sense of sight their subjective sense. What might seem odd, given what we have just said about the two types, is that our names for the two types are not reversed. But our reason for naming them as do will shortly appear. What I think should be clear, or should be becoming clear, is that these two types, the tt and vt, are the vice versa of each other.

But where, it will be asked, did we get this typology? As indicated above, most importantly from the history of philosophy. But in the first instance, it was gotten from difficulties that I, DB, had understanding what Berkeley says about his experience of sight and touch in his NTV.

That forced me to look closely at my own experience, which seemed so different from his. This was the first stage in the development of the Tactual Visual Typology (TVT). The next phase was looking at the history of philosophy for those philosophers who had written on the subject to see if they could help me deal with my difficulties. And what I found, especially in Locke and Abbott, among others, did help me, and enabled me to formulate a rough typal division, with Berkeley, Locke and Kant on one side, and Russell, Abbott and myself on the other. Another stage was to question colleagues and philosophy students, in one-to-one discussions, to see how far their experiences fitted with my preliminary findings about the two types.[8] The result of all this was the Tactual Visual Typology, or TVT, as presented in my unpublished 2010 work, called the 'Penult', which I made available to students in the Philosophy Dept, and which condensed and significantly revised is now presented in this section.

#3a: Locke

According to Locke, solidity is the core quality of matter, its primary primary quality, which, according to him, is known through the sense of touch (see *Essay* II.iii.2). For as he nicely puts it at the end of his chapter 'Of solidity' (*Essay* II.iv.6):

> If any one asks me, What this Solidity is, I send him to his Senses to inform him: Let him put a Flint, or a Foot-ball between his Hands; and then endeavour to join them, and he will know.

So the sensory experience of touching or pressing or feeling resistance is, according to Locke, how we know solidity, and hence a material object. Of course, Locke is aware that most people think they also see solidity. But this, he believes, is a mistake. That it is not sight that brings us into contact with solidity comes out in the following searching passage from *Essay* II.ix.8. Here, Locke explains that what we actually or immediately see when, for example, we think we see a convex object of uniform colour is actually a

> flat circle variously shadow'd, with several degrees of light and brightness coming to our eyes. But we having by use been accustomed to perceive, what kind of appearance convex bodies are wont to make in us; what alterations are made in the reflections of light, by the difference of the sensible figures of

the bodies, the judgment presently, by an habitual custom, alters the appearances into their causes: so from that, which truly is variety of shadow or colour, [the judgment] … frames to it self the perception of a convex figure, and an uniform colour, when the idea [or sensation] we receive from thence, is only a plain variously coloured, as is evident in painting.

There is a lot in this passage. And I think that Berkeley drew importantly on it in his NTV. Locke's main point is that our mistake is based on confusing what we immediately see with what we very quickly infer from that immediate experience; and that it is like the way we see depth in a painting, which while really only a plane or two-dimensional can, if skillfully executed by an artist, make us think we see solid objects. But the key thing is that for Locke we don't see solid material things, but we feel them. From this it follows that if we had only sight, or lacked touch, we should not experience solid material objects in space.

Locke says little by way of justifying why he believes that he touches material things. Locke seems to take it that it is evident that the feeling of resistance proves that he is in contact with external physical things, and that physical things are tangible. However, there can be little doubt that he was also being influenced by the scientific theory developed by the great leaders of modern science, by Galileo, Descartes, Newton and Boyle, that material things are constituted by what Locke called the primary qualities, such as solidity, extension, number, which are known by touch, and not by sight or hearing, tasting and smelling, which senses only bring us into contact with what Locke called the secondary qualities, which are not actually in material things.

#3b: Russell

We now move to Russell who is not as direct as Locke; hence we have to do some unpacking and sorting to be clear about his position. But here we are working with one of Russell's best known and most lucid works, his *Problems of Philosophy*, 1912. Russell begins by taking an empirical example, his brown writing table, which becomes his paradigmatic material object.

Russell first considers what he sees and spends a lot of time on the colour of the table, noting that although we would be naturally inclined to say it is simply and only brown, more careful scrutiny shows that its colour varies, depending on how the light falls on it, for sometimes it is shimmering dark and light patches. Russell then moves to texture, which he still talks about as being seen. And the conclusion he comes to with respect to texture is the one he reached with respect to colour: that it varies, for while it seems to be uniform, if we were to look at it under a microscope the texture would be very different, having hills and valleys, just as the colour of the table changes with different lighting conditions. Russell then considers the shape of the table, which he again examines within the modality of sight and concludes that it 'is no better' than the previous qualities of colour and texture. In short, it is also variable.

Having been in the modality of sight for three pages, Russell then moves to touch and hearing, both of which he covers in one paragraph. He also describes the data of touch in a different way. Unlike that of sight, he describes what he experiences by touch as sensations: sensations of hardness. And these sensations, he says, vary in similar ways to colour, texture and shape, depending on the degree of pressure we exert when feeling or pressing against the table. That what he experiences by touch is clearly sensations, he seems to think is evident and need not be argued for. 'And the same [he says] applies still more obviously to the sounds which can be elicited by rapping the table.'

Now it is the difference between sight and touch that we need to focus on, for these are the two key senses, it is widely agreed, that are supposed to bring us in contact with material things. But before getting to that, we need to quickly make explicit the conclusion Russell reaches from his preceding introspective experiences and arguments. This is that we do not truly experience material things, such as his table, by sense. For the material table is supposed to be a thing that has fixed qualities, but that is not what Russell found from experience; for Russell thinks his experience has shown that the sensory qualities of the table are variable and relative.

So Russell concludes that 'the real table, if there is one, is not known to us at all' by direct experience, but must be inferred. So realism, according to which we directly sense material things, is mistaken. What we directly experience are sensations and not material things.

But this does not show that immaterialism is true, according to Russell, rather he thinks that materialistic representationalism is true; so what we experience only represents the material world. Also, more specifically, Russell maintains that sensations are not mental, which, according to Russell, Berkeley wrongly thought they were and which premise he used to justify his immaterialism. Russell believes they are not mental because no objects for Russell are mental. The mental, according to Russell (i.e. of 1912–1917) is, following Moore, restricted to mental acts, not to the objects of mental acts.[9]

So in 1912 Russell rejects realism but also immaterialism and idealism, which is the positive side of immaterialism. However, what is important for us comes when he hones in on the question why we believe in matter. The key passage needs to be quoted and looked at carefully:

Of course it is not by argument that we originally come by our belief in an independent external world. We find this belief already in ourselves as soon as we begin to reflect: it is what may be called an instinctive belief. [However] We should never have been led to question that belief but for the fact that, at any rate in the case of sight, it seems as if the sense-datum itself were instinctively believed to be the independent object, whereas argument shows that the object cannot be identical with the sense-datum.

So for Russell, we believe in an independent material world instinctively. But our confidence in this instinctive belief is brought into question in a curious way, Russell suggests, by our sense of sight. For sight seems to bring us immediately and directly in contact with material objects, hence is close to being instinctive, and certainly closer than the other four senses. But when sight is examined carefully, as Russell does, then its apparent ability to bring us into direct and immediate contact with material objects is brought into question. What Russell is saying is that while we instinctively and rightly believe that material objects exist independently of us, and that the sense of sight seems to confirm and go along with this, yet when we realize that sight does not bring us into immediate contact with material things, we feel let down, and question the truthfulness of the instinct itself. But Russell thinks this is a mistake. For the 'discovery' that we don't experience physical things but only sensations, even in the case of sight, 'which is not at all paradoxical in the case of taste, smell and sound, and only slightly so in the case of touch – leaves [or should leave] undiminished our instinctive belief that there are objects corresponding to our sense data'.

The key point that I want to make is that for Russell it is the sense of sight, and not touch, which he thinks makes us believe that we directly and immediately experience external material things, whereas for Locke it is touch that does so, and truly does so. To be sure, Russell does say that touch does somewhat foster a belief in external objects, but not nearly as strongly as sight. For Russell seems clear that his touching gives tactual sensations. And that, taken together with what he says about seeing, shows he was a tt.

#3c: Kant and Dr Johnson

We now move to Kant, who, fortunately, on this subject is more straightforward than Russell, and is nearly as easy to follow as Locke. Here the crucial work is Kant's *Anthropology from a Pragmatic Point of View* (1798), especially sections 17 and 19, which are on the senses of touch and sight respectively. For Kant, the sense of touch is

> the only one of *immediate* [Kant's italics] external perception; and for this very reason it is also the most important and most reliably instructive, but nevertheless it is the coarsest, because the matter

whose surface is to inform us about the shape of the object through touching must be solid. ... Without this sense organ we would be unable to form any concept at all of a bodily shape ... '

(section 17)

So touch more than any of the senses brings us in contact with external objects, or as Kant also says, stirs up '*cognition* of the external object', rather than 'consciousness of the affected organ' (p. 47), i.e. sensation.

Kant also makes the shrewd observation that we human beings are able to form an adequate concept of shape because of the construction of our fingers, which are able to touch and hold a body 'on all sides'.

So like Locke, but more comprehensively, touch is for Kant the sense that brings us into direct contact with material objects. And this is confirmed by what Kant says of sight, which he describes as a 'sense of *mediate* sensation'.

What is initially puzzling, however, is that although Kant regards sight as not bringing us into contact with material things, he regards sight as vastly superior in other respects to touch and also hearing. For, as he says,

By means of sight the cosmos becomes known to us to an extent so immeasurable that ... we become fatigued over the long number of sequence. And this almost gives us more reason to be astonished at the delicate sensitivity of this organ ... especially when we take in the world in detail, as ... through the mediation of the microscope ... The sense of sight ... is still the noblest, because of all the senses it is the furthest removed from the sense of touch, the most limited ...

(section 19)

So touch is the 'coarsest' and the 'most limited' sense, but without it we would have no grasp of external objects: we would be locked up in sensation. Therefore, while sight is more dispensable than touch or hearing, it is nonetheless superior in important ways. Working through light, which is a medium that 'spreads itself in space in all directions', sight has more delicate sensitivity, more scope, more detail. Hence Kant calls sight the 'noblest sense' and touch the 'most limited'.

Although Kant is famous as a theoretician, I suggest that here he is working, at least partly, from his own immediate sensory experience. And what it shows is that his experience was different from Russell's but was like that of Locke, that he was a vt, rather than, like Russell, a tt. So his intimate direct experience was far more in his seeing, in the delicacy of his visual sensations. However, again there is the question whether when Kant talks about his touching material things he, like Locke, was being at least partly influenced by the primary-secondary quality distinction, accepted by science, that solid material things are tangible. Here the principle is that type is shown by what an individual immediately and intimately experiences, which was for Kant the delicacy of visual sensations, and this also comes out in what Kant says about art, especially about music.

Thus in section 28, Kant says that 'there are more people than one would believe who have a good and even extremely sensitive sense of hearing, but who have absolutely no musical ear; whose sense for tone is entirely indifferent not merely to imitating tones (singing) but also distinguishing them from noise.' I think it is likely that Kant had himself in mind here, and this is supported by what he says in the *Critique of Aesthetic Judgment*, pp. 195–198, where he expresses a low opinion of music, observing, for example, that music lacks 'urbanity' in scattering sounds 'through the neighborhood, and thus, as it were, becomes obtrusive and deprives others, outside the musical circle, of their freedom'.

Drawing on Kant, I think we can now be clearer about how to distinguish a vt from a tt. If someone sees or touches an object such that the experience seems to be coming from the sense organ, then that is not their objective sense, yet it shows the person's sensory type. So it seems that, given what Kant says, that what he immediately experienced he saw in his eyes. And, as he puts it in section 19, such experiences are likely to be intense, in which case, he also says, it is harder 'to find the concept of the object'. Instead we have the sensation or the 'organic sensation', which is something more aesthetic and pleasurable or painful. For Kant, this describes seeing. For me, as a tt, it describes touching.

Here is another although more indirect way of picking out a vt and confirming that Kant was one. The evidence is from Kant's discussion of imagination (in section 28) and on the aesthetic delight of the individual senses, where he himself almost seems to be paving the way to the kind of topology I am developing here. As against the Typical Mind Fallacy, or TMF, he notes that there are surprising and basic differences between people in their sensing. Thus he observes that some people are totally colour-blind and have only the experience of black and white, and therefore see the world 'like a copperplate engraving'. He then says 'that the same may be true with the ideas of taste and smell', that there are people who don't enjoy the objects of these senses, although presumably they can discriminate in practical or functional ways in the senses in question. He also observes, as mentioned above, that there are some people who are indifferent to the sound of music or cannot distinguish it from noise. But it is also interesting that he omits the sense of sight here. So he doesn't seem to think that anyone with normal visual discrimination could lack aesthetic enjoyment in the visual sense. And this is what one would expect of a strong vt, who – falling into the TMF – would consider the enjoyment of shapes, patterns and especially colours to be a natural or universal human capacity. But it isn't. And I know this because I am myself in the lower end of the visual enjoyment continuum.

Here, then, we have an important indicator of sensory type. For there is evidence that Berkeley also had virtually no appreciation of music, whereas he did very much enjoy visual art and natural visual beauty. According to his biographer, Joseph Stock, he is reported as saying: 'I have eyes but no ears.' On the other hand, music for me is the one art which literally moves me, giving me the greatest pleasure as well as my understanding of beauty, whereas I have virtually no appreciation of painting or natural beauty, that is, scenery.

Another notable individual who was like Berkeley and Kant in this respect was Dr Johnson. Thus we know from Boswell's *Life of Johnson*, 1791, that Johnson had little or no appreciation of music. And from Boswell's account of Johnson's famous 'refutation' of Berkeley's immaterialism, it also seems clear that Johnson was a vt. For, according to Boswell, the way Johnson believed he had refuted Berkeley was by 'striking his foot with mighty force against a large stone, till he rebounded from it'. So what Johnson did with his foot to be assured that matter exists is what Locke suggested could be done by someone using his hands and pressing them against a football to feel its resistance.[10]

#3d: T. K. Abbott

We now move to T. K. Abbott, who is much less well known than the three philosophers I have examined above. Yet he was a person of considerable accomplishment, indeed a polymath, who was Professor of Moral Philosophy at Trinity College Dublin, also a Hebrew and Greek scholar and translator of Kant's second *Critique*. But Abbott's main claim to fame in philosophy was his 1864 book, *Sight and Touch*, in which he attacks Berkeley's theory of vision.

Here I want to show how extreme and pure Abbott was as a tt; which fits with his being sure that Berkeley was wrong in his theory of vision. The reason is that Abbott's own direct sensory experience was so opposed to Berkeley's. Abbott is clearest at the beginning of chap. V, where he writes: 'Touch gives us nothing but a series of sensations which have of themselves no more connexion with extension than with colour.' Abbott then criticizes Alexander Bain's theory that locomotion is a tactual experience which gives externality; whereas for Abbott it is no more than 'muscular exertion' (p. 61). And as Abbott says elsewhere, p. 69: 'Extension has three dimensions [like material objects]; whereas muscular effort has only one. The parts of extension are co-existent [by which I think he means spatial]; those of muscular effort are successive [therefore only in time].'

So for Abbott, 'touch itself cannot give the idea of anything beyond or without us, since for touch nothing has any existence which is not actually in contact with the surface of the body.' Abbott uses the example of the position of his toe, by which, he writes, we must mean the toe's position relative to the other parts of his body, for place is a relative idea. But, he writes:

> we are not conscious of the size of the toe, or its form, or its distance from the centre. All sensations are in fact central [i.e. not in any part of the body, but experienced in the mind] and it is only by association that we learn to refer certain sensations to certain external visible and tangible organs.
>
> (p. 62)

(Note that when he speaks of being 'conscious of the size of the toe', in the first sentence, he must mean conscious by feeling, so he probably is supposing that his toe is in his shoe and so can't be seen.)

For as Abbott says:

> When I say then that I feel a pain in my foot, I am not stating a fact of consciousness but an inference. The part in which I feel the pain is known to consciousness only as the seat of such sensations. I

infer from association that the source of the pain is in a certain visual tangible part of the body.

(pp. 63–4)

Here I should note that all of this very closely fits my own experience, which I believe is typical of the tt.

Abbott also draws on the evidence of the blind from birth – from Platner who says that 'touch alone conveys no knowledge of what belongs to external space, knows nothing of local separation; and in a word, the blind man perceives absolutely nothing of the external world … ' (p. 73). For further evidence of Abbott's tt experience and type, see pp. 10, 28–29, 35–38, 75, 80.

#4: The valley and hills model

Having presented the four exemplary philosophers, and the data which identifies them as either tt or vt, I now want to present a model for identifying different kinds or levels of the tt and vt type.

The model is the bell curve, but turned upside down, so it is seen as a valley between two hills. Now everyone in the valley believes that they and everyone else perceive material things by both sight and touch. Those in the valley can be called the valley folk. But just as individual human beings are not fully symmetrical in their bodies, so some valley folk are more inclined to believe that their sight brings them into contact with material things and some that it is their touch that does so. Imagine then that the former are on the left side of the valley and the latter on the right side. Going further, we can then imagine that some individuals do, at times, climb up one or the other hillside, and remain there for a time. These are psychologists and/or philosophers, who have decided views on the senses of sight and touch and can be called the hill folk. The hill folk on the left believe that it is touch more than sight that brings them and everyone else into contact with material things. Then there are those at summit of the hill who believe that it is only touch that does so. It is there that we would find Locke and Kant. And on the other hill we find those holding the vice versa view. Hence it is on that hill side that we would find Russell, although he believes that sight only seems to bring him into contact with material things, for no sense does that, whereas Abbott holds that sight does bring him into contact with material things, hence he is on the right hand summit and is the vice versa of Locke and Kant.

More generally, what our model shows are three ways or levels of being a vt or tt: as valley folk, hill folk and those on the summit. But what also needs to be observed is that there have always been, and still are, far more folk on the left hillside. Also that until the nineteenth century, it seems that there was no one at the summit of the right hill. Why was this so? Is it because there are more who experience in the vt way in the population than in the tt way, so more vt than tt? I do not think so. Rather, I think it is because there are other factors or reasons at work. One, as mentioned above, is that the vt position is in accord with the scientific view as expressed in the primary-secondary quality distinction. The belief in the primacy of the tactual over the visual also fits with the fact that humans need tangible food for nourishment in order to live. So the tactual, much more than the visual, needs to be attended to, since tactuality also involves dangers, for some tactuality is dangerous to life, for example, being pounded by speeding truck, whereas few if any visual sense data are so important. For while strong light can dazzle and hurt the eyes, it cannot endanger life, as strong tactual pressures can. The primacy and reliability of the tactual over the visual are also shown in the fact that nearly all sensory illusions are in the sense of sight, and that there are very few in the modality of touch. This shows that there is much more chance of being deceived in the sense of sight than in the sense of touch, which could be more serious in a practical way than being deceived in the sense sight.

These I think are the reasons that up to the nineteenth century, there were few, if any, on the right hill side and no one at its summit. Nor, given this, is it surprising that those on right hillside folk, like Locke and Kant, literally looked down on the valley folk, who believed that material things are known by both senses. However, one psychologist and philosopher who did come forward to speak for the valley folk was Samuel Bailey, who, in his 1842 *Review of Berkeley Theory of Vision* opposed the generally accepted view of philosophers and psychologists and argued that material things are perceived by both sight and touch. So Bailey begins the process of questioning the hegemony of those on left hill side. But Abbott, to his credit, goes even further in opposing Berkeley and those on the left in his 1864 work; and he seems to have been the first tt to appear on the summit of the hill on the right.

Perhaps the main thing we wish to make clear in our model and discussion above is that what identifies the two types, as we understand them, is not their reasons but their experience. In this respect, Abbott is clearest; for while he does have some reasons for believing that he as well as other human beings do not perceive material things by touch, what most convinces him is his experience. So it is experience, either of the tt or vt kind, that identifies type.

#5: The role of imagery and normal synaesthesia

Now having identified the two types more clearly in the previous section by distinguishing and putting aside the non-experiential factors which caused especially the vt to believe that material things are known by touch, Neo-B and I now want to suggest a way of explaining how and why the tt and vt experience in the distinctive ways they do. (Here I should note that strictly for ease and simplicity of expression, I shall refer to the vt as 'she' and the tt as 'he'.) This is that a vt believes her touching most confidently brings her into contact with material things, because she unconsciously projects strong visual imagery into what she actually touches and feels, thereby structuring and embodying it, making her believe that she is touching something solid and experiencing a material object. But she is not aware of doing this. She is only aware of the outcome of her projection.

However, the vt believes she can indirectly confirm that she feels material things, and does not see them, because she is able to understand that what she immediately and directly sees, as Locke explains, is a two-dimensional array of light and colours. And some vt are able, to a great extent and if they wish, to experience what they immediately see as two-dimensional and flat, which the vt believes confirms that it is not her seeing, but her touching, that brings her in contact with solid external material things.

Here I should note that this account of the mechanism whereby the vt converts what she touches into solid material things, by projecting visual imagery, is based in large measure on the scientific fact, which was first discovered by Francis Galton, that some individuals are strong and others weak in producing visual images.[11]

Neo-B and I have then been able to correlate the strong imagers with the vt and the weak imagers with tt. And no doubt the most important correlation for the development of the typology was that I, DB, knew myself to be a weak imager, whereas I knew that Berkeley was a strong imager (see Berman 2008).

Going further, we know that a strong imager, like Berkeley, is able (as he says in PHK section 28) to do things with his images, as for example combine them in various ways, which a weak imager like myself is unable to do. Hence it is not surprising that a strong imager is able to do things with what she actually sees, so see it as 2D or convert it from 3D to 2D, which is evidence that the strong imager and the vt overlap at least to a great extent. We say 'to a great extent' because we have evidence that some strong imagers are not visual types; hence we are not equating the strong imager and the vt.

The tt, on the other hand, is the vice versa of the vt. So he is a weak imager, who is strong in the modality of touch, by which we mean that he can, if he wishes and to a great extent or completely, experience what he touches as tactual sense data. For because he is likely to have little or no capacity for imaging, what he is able to experience by touch is not very much, or not at all, structured and objectified by the unconscious projection of imagery into it – as is the case with the vt – but can be experienced as raw tactual data.

However, as we understand it, this is a matter of degree. Thus we know at least one very strong tt who is a total non-imager (see note 8), and other strong tt who are weak imagers and other tt who are somewhat stronger imagers, these getting close to weak vt.

So the strongest tt, who are likely to have little or no imaging ability, are able to recognize that all they immediately feel or touch are tactual sensations. And this, as we have seen, was the case with Abbott, although we do not know what Abbott's imaging ability was. Russell was also a strong tt, but as he believed that touch did, to some extent, make him believe he was touching material things, he was not as strong a tt as Abbott. However, Russell was still a strong tt, since he is clear that it is sight, and not touch, that most forcibly makes him (wrongly) believe that he is in contact with material things. And we have good evidence that Russell was a weak imager.

Neo-B then goes one step further in explaining the different experiences of the tt and vt, by introducing a new theory. This is the theory of normal synaesthesia. Here it is necessary to say a word about the phenomenon of synaesthesia. In its most striking form, synaesthesia, or syn for short, is a cross-modal condition in which, for example, someone listening to music hears the musical sounds as shapes. But only a small percentage of the population have such a condition. The way Neo-B uses synaesthesia concerns all human beings. But how then can Neo-B's explanation explain what everyone experiences by drawing on synaesthesia? Because Neo-B holds that there are two kinds of synaesthesia, one normal synaesthesia, the other anomalous. Yet what is happening in the experience of both is essential synthaesthetic. Thus just as an anomalous synesthete can't not hear certain music as visual shapes, so the tt, as normal synaesthete, can't not see the visual as tangible when he sees what is visual. (And he also finds it hard to believe that what he touches is not also visual; but in this case he is able to overcome the difficulty.)

Yet Neo-B and I are clear that what a tt is immediately seeing is only visual, just as the synaesthete who believes he sees music is really only hearing sounds. And one reason we believe this is that, like Berkeley, we believe there is no overlapping of the senses of sight or touch. So what we all, tt and vt, see with our eyes is only visual. For the eyes do not touch or feel. And what we all touch with our hands is not seen, since hands cannot see, they can only touch or feel. So we agree with Berkeley about the heterogeneity of sight and touch. But this is not what realists and materialists believe.

And Neo-B and I accept that what most people – the valley folk – believe is that they both see and touch material things. What is rarer is that some individuals think that it is either sight or touch that most convinces them and us of material things, or that it is only either sight or only touch that brings them into contact with material things. They are extremists – either hill folk or those at the summit – and not primarily in their reasoning or theory, if they are tt or vt, but in their experience. Yet in their normal, practical activity in the world, even they believe that they both see and touch material objects. However, as we have observed above, what makes this more complicated is that a vt also believes that it is only touch that brings her and other human beings into contact with material things because she is convinced by the theory of primary secondary qualities, and/or because she recognizes that touch is practically most important, even necessary, for human life, which is not the case with sight, despite its enormous practical and aesthetic value. What Neo-B and I are interested in is only her experience, not her reasons, for it is her experience alone that identifies her vt type. The tt are less complicated than the vt in this respect because there is little or no theory and reason which supports the tt belief that he only sees material things and does not touch them.

#6: The Maupertius move

Now we need to come to the main philosophical conclusion which Neo-B draws from his TVT. This is the conclusion he reaches by consulting those who have the purest experience of what is seen and touched, so those at the two hill summits, who are there because of their respective experiences, and so are either extreme and pure tt or extreme and pure vt. What Neo-B then finds in his discussions with such vt is that they believe that material objects exist because they touch them but they firmly deny that they see them. For what they say they immediately see are visual sense-data [= s-d]. And what Neo-B finds from his discussions with the tt is that they believe material objects exist because they see them, but they confidently deny they touch them, since by touch they experience only tactual s-d. Now what Neo-B takes most seriously in his discussions with the vt and tt is not what they affirm but what they deny. And the conclusion that Neo-B draws from this is that neither the vt or the tt experience material things. What they both experience is only s-d. More specifically, Neo-B sees each type as like a precision scientific instrument when the tt is experiencing by touch, and when the vt experiencing by sight. But, of course, the tt believes he sees material things and the vt believes that she touches material things. But there Neo-B thinks they are both wrong because both are deceived by their normal synaesthesis. And they can know this, Neo-B holds, by their ability to de-syn in the alternative sense. For having introduced normal syn, Neo-B also introduces the activity of de-syning. This is an activity whereby a tt can, by focussed effort and in certain conditions, be aware that what he is actually directly and immediately feeling is not a material object, but only tactual s-d. Hence he can realize, with Neo-B's help, that what makes the vt hill folk (mistakenly) believe they touch material things is their normal synaesthesia, which is brought about by their projecting visual imagery into what they feel.

The very strong tt can know this, because when, for example, he feels a coin in his pocket, he is able to recognize that there is a visual image hovering in the background wanting to connect with his actual tactual sensations and structure it in such a way as to make him believe he is feeling a solid material coin. But he can stop it from doing so, because his visual imagery is weak. But this is not the case with the vt, whose visual imagery is strong. So that is the reason, according to Neo-B, why she believes she is feeling material things. The tt is happy with this, but not happy when Neo-B goes on to apply this to the tt experience of seeing. For by parity of reasoning, Neo-B explains to the tt that he believes he sees material things because he is projecting his strong tactual imagery into what he actually sees, that is visual s-d. And the reason this must be done is that material things must be believed in, since the belief is so useful and indeed necessary.

And Neo-B then uses the vice versa argument in his discussion with the extremely strong vt, who is at the summit of the left hill. Putting this in another way, what Neo-B thinks he can show is that the tt is right about what he denies but wrong about what he affirms. Thus he is right about his experience of what he took to be his subjective sense, but wrong about what he took to be his objective sense. For in the latter case it was a mediated judgement, not direct experience. And the same applies to the vt. So Neo-B tells each that what they should rely on is what they directly and immediately experience, for it is most evident.

What Neo-B is working on is that the vt and tt themselves are convinced of what they deny through their de-syning experiments, namely the tt's denial that he or everyone else is able to experience material things by touch, and the vt's denial that she or everyone can experience material things by sight. So they see that de-syning experiments are destructive against the opposing type's belief in material things. They see the mote in the eye of the opposing type, but do not see the beam in their own. But Neo-B hopes that he can show this to them, and that they should then accept that material things are not experienced by either sight or touch, that all that both sight and touch present are s-d.

So each type is right about what it denies, but wrong about what it affirms.

And in order to capture this crucial truth in a memorable and dramatic way Neo-B introduces what he call the Maupertius move. It is called the Maupertius move, because of a story about the first meeting between Voltaire and P. L. Maupertius, another luminary of the Enlightenment. The story goes that after the meeting, someone asked Voltaire what he thought of Maupertius, to which Voltaire said that he thought Maupertius was a man of great and solid learning as well as a gentleman. But noticing that this elicited a curious smile, Voltaire then asked his interrogator: And what did Maupertius think of me? To which came to the reply, To be honest, he thought you were a fool, to which Voltaire said, after a moment's reflection: Well, probably we were both mistaken.

That is also what Neo-B and I want to say of and to the tt and vt: that they are both mistaken in what they accept to be true, that matter exists, but right in what each denies, that, according to the vt, sight does not bring us into contact with material things, and, according to the tt, touch does not bring us into contact with material things. Hence the conclusion, according to Neo-B, is that phenomenalism is true, according to which, as J. S. Mill famously puts it, what exists is the 'permanent possibility of sensation', that is, especially tactual and visual sensations, but also the sensations of the three other senses. Although Neo-B also adds that dualist and monist minds also exist, as well as the tt and vt types of experiencing.

However, here we need to focus on that part of our argument where the tt and vt are right, namely that what they do or can directly and immedately experience are s-d, the tt of tactual s-d, the vt of visual s-d. The crucial idea is that what is immediately and directly experienced is most certain. Similarly what are also certain are self-evident propositions or axioms, such as A=A, or that I know that I exist.

To be sure, Neo-B and I do not expect that our TVT and argument for phenomenalism are going to be accepted without opposition. And prima facie, there do seem to be problems. One is that it seems to go against science, which believes that matter exists and that it is largely tactual, that is, mass. Here I can only say a word in response, namely that phenomenalism has been regarded by serious scientists, such as Ernst Mach and the early Einstein, as a feasible basis for science.

However there is a second, deeper difficulty that needs to be faced. This is that if what actually exists are only a changing array of light and colour sensations and raw tactual s-d, then it seems to reverse what is understood as the subjective and objective, making our sensations objective and material objects subjective. But if that is so, then perceiving and knowing the truth is useless and indeed dangerous. For perceiving and knowing the world as visual and tactual s-d, rather than material objects, cannot help us to operate or survive in the world. We might as well be without sight and touch. Therefore accepting the TVT seems to turn the world upside down. We think it does, but while we think it should be accepted as true, we think it need not and should not be accepted as the way we should live. We should live as the valley people do, believing that we both see and touch material objects. So we should believe or act on what we know to be false.

#7: Berkeley on the vt summit

With the Maupertius Move, Neo-B is addressing the strong tt and vt and trying to show each that it is right about what it denies but wrong about what it affirms. But neither does Neo-B forget the valley folk, who believe that matter is known by both sight and touch. And, as mentioned, we are all valley folk, because that is where and the way we normally live and operate. And, as just mentioned, the valley folk are right to live and operate in this way, according to Neo-B, but it is still wrong to believe it is true. To show this, Neo-B can bring in Samuel Bailey again, as probably the first philosopher of the valley folk. For, as mentioned above, in his 1842 *Review*, Bailey holds that we perceive material things by both sight AND touch, so he opposes both the tt and especially vt, because they were dominant at the time. And one way that he justifies his realist and materialist position is by means of what might be called the mirror argument. Bailey uses it to prove, as against the vt, that it is in the nature of the sense of sight to see material objects at a distance. And this he says can be proved by looking into a mirror. For, he maintains,

> No touching or handling can cause us to see the images reflected in the [looking] glass to be on its surface. We see them beyond the surface and cannot even imagine them otherwise.

> (p. 62)

So Bailey thinks that Locke and Berkeley in the NTV are wrong. But it is Bailey who is wrong, because I know a number of individuals who are sure they can see their images as on the surface of a mirror. They can do it, but they need to make an effort to do so, for their normal experience is seeing the images as having depth. That was Bailey's experience and is my own, for I am a tt. What Bailey failed to realize is that there is another type, the vt, and that strong vt can do what he says is impossible. To be sure, Bailey might say that they think they can do it, but really they are deceiving themselves. But what the strong vt have said or written to me about their experience is, I think, convincing in its detail. Thus one wrote to me that when she does the mirror experience her experience is like the duck-rabbit, that she can see either depth or flatness, that what she sees flits from one to the other.

Moreover, I think there is also evidence that a strong vt can go further and see her visual field as not merely flat, or composed of shapes on a flat surface, but as only diverse colours. Thus in his NTV, section 157, Berkeley says:

it seems to be the opinion of some ingenious men, that flat or plain figures are immediate objects of sight, though they acknowledge solids are not. And this opinion of theirs is grounded on what is observed in painting, [Here I think Berkeley must surely be referring to Locke's *Essay* II.ix.8.] wherein (say they) the ideas immediately imprinted on the mind are only of planes variously coloured, which by a sudden act of the judgement are changed into solids: But, with a little attention we shall find the planes here mentioned, as the immediate objects of sight, are not visible, but tangible plains. For when we say that pictures are plains: we mean thereby, that they appear to the touch smooth and uniform. But then this smoothness and uniformity, or, in other words, this planeness of the picture, is not perceived immediately by vision: For it appeareth to the eye various and multiform.

I think Berkeley is here doing very careful and rigorous sensory introspection, moreso than Locke. For I think he is, in effect, saying that Locke's vt account of his experience did not go far enough, that not only are there no solids things that can be seen, but also no flat things, because neither can be seen, for both can only be touched or felt.

For Berkeley then concludes

… for planes are no more the immediate object of sight than solids. [That] What we strictly see are not solids, nor yet planes variously coloured; they are only diversity of colours. … So that we see planes, in the same way that we see solids; both being equally suggested by the immediate objects of sight, which accordingly are themselves denominated planes and solids: But though they are called by the same names with the things marked by them, they are nevertheless of a nature entirely different ...

(section 158)

However, in section 159, the last section of the NTV, Berkeley concedes that it takes considerable pains and effort to separate

in our thoughts the proper objects of sight from those of touch which are connected with them. This, indeed, in a complete degree, seems scarce possible to be performed: Which will not seem strange to us, if we consider how hard it is, for any one to hear the words of his native language pronounced in his ears without understanding them. Though he endeavour to disunite the meaning from the sound, it will nevertheless intrude into his thoughts, and he shall find it extremely difficult, if not impossible, to put himself exactly in the posture of a foreigner, that never learned the language, so as to be affected barely with the sounds themselves, and not perceive the signification annexed to them.

Berkeley's point is that what we immediately hear when we hear someone speaking to us in our native language are just sounds or phonemes. But we find it almost impossible to experience this, and not straightaway understand what is meant by the words. So here in Berkeley's analogy from language we have an excellent illustration of the normal synaesthesia of the visual type. So Locke's seeing planes was an example of normal synaesthesia, but more searching than seeing solids, which is more normal. And Neo-B would also want to say that the same analysis needs to be applied, mutatis mutandis, to the very strong tactual type, that he finds it hard to experience what he actually sees are only visual s-d and not material things, although somewhat easier to recognize that what he touches or feels are only tactual s-d and not material things.

However, a key question, for our purpose, is whether Berkeley was able to experience what he touched or felt as just 'diversity' of tactual sensations. For it could be that he holds this from reasoning, so from theory. And this would fit with the thought experiment that provides the context of what he is saying, namely that of the unbodied person, that is, the person with no sense of touch. But we believe that probably no living person could be without some sense of touch, and if so the experiment would not be possible for a living human being. And if that is the case, then Berkeley could not experience just diversity of tactual sensations. So I think Berkeley probably did not have the experience, but I think he might have thought that if he worked hard enough at it he could have that experience.

………… …..

One final point we want to make is that Berkeley also comes very close to Neo-B on the TVT; hence that we are justified in seeing the TVT as truly Neo-Berkeleian. For, as we know, Berkeley's position in the NTV was strategic. His actual position was what he puts forward in the PHK, which is that not only do we not see material things, but we also do not feel them, because material objects do not exist. Hence tangible material things do not exist, so what we feel are only tactual s-d. Therefore, only s-d exists in the object world. This is also Neo-B's view as shown in the Maupertius Move. The one difference is that Neo-B believes actual Berkeley is mistaken in seeing s-d as dependent on minds for their existence. On this, Neo-B goes along with Hume's and Mill's phenomenalism, and not with Berkeley's idealism. Although, as we have also seen in part one, Neo-B rejects Hume's claim that minds distinct from s-d do not exist. Berkeley also gets close to the TVT in 1733 in holding that while material things do not exist, it is useful to believe in them. So for Berkeley it is God who, in his goodness, is responsible for normal synaesthesia and the useful belief that material things are both seen and touched. Where Berkeley differs most from Neo-B and the TVT is not seeing the centrality of types.

… …

NOTES

Part 1

1 See *Works*, vol. 8, p. 16. Also see below, part two, section 2 and Berman 1994, pp. 22–9.

2 To be sure, it could be argued that *De Motu* stands on its own from Berkeley's other philosophical works, as being written for a particular purpose and directed to a certain audience. Hence his emphatic dualistic assertions should not be taken too seriously. Yet this is belied by the fact that in his letter of November 1729, to his American friend, Samuel Johnson, Berkeley recommends his *De Motu;* also that he reprinted it in his *Miscellany*, without making any changes to it, and that he commends *De Motu* in *Siris*, section 250.

3 Also see my *Consciousness from Descartes to A. J. Ayer*, forthcoming from Palgrave Macmillan.

4 Goldsmith tells the story in his 1759 Memoir of Berkeley. For details, see Berman (1994, Epilogue).

5 Here I need to emphasize that in his early works Berkeley did not at all accept that it was God who was behind the general belief in material objects. Thus in PHK, section 54, he even questioned whether there was such a belief; and in DHP, he has Philonous categorically assert that 'I do not suppose God has deceived man at all' with respect to material things. But Berkeley changed his mind on this by 1733, as shown in section 36 of the TVV, since I take it that those who believe that they see and touch one thing are believing that they are perceiving material things, and that Berkeley recognized this.

Part 2

6 Pantheism, as in Spinoza, is a third system, according to which there is only one mind, namely the Infinite Mind of God, but unlike God in the Christian or Monotheistic system, the one God of pantheism is not distinct from the world, and that is why Spinoza speaks of Deus sive Natura, that is, God or Nature. As Neo-B sees it, Pantheism and Polytheism are more likely to be true than Monotheism, which is a mistaken compromise between them. Monotheism is also the latecomer, emerging scarcely more than 2000 years ago as widely held; but then, when once taken from Judaism, proving a popular compromise, first in Christianity, then in Islam.

7 Of course, the monist cannot have this loving or intimate experience with another individual, since for the monist there is only one individual, God or Nature, as Spinoza says. But according to Neo-B, Spinoza and other monists can have the monistic counterpart of the dualistic intimacy in being in accord with the mind of God, which Spinoza discusses at the end of his *Ethics*, which could be called monistic intimacy.

8 For one such discussion, see my *Manual of Experimental Philosophy*, especially pp. 69–70. This was with Prof Timo Airaksinen of the University of Helsinki, who is a strong tt and a non-imager.

9 On Russell's change of mind in 1918 and rejection of the act-object distinction, see my *Manual*, pp. 99–101.

10 See *Life of Johnson*, end of year 1763 for Dr Johnson's stone-kicking refutation of Berkeley's immaterialism. In the year 1777, Boswell records that Johnson 'owned to me that he was very insensible to the power of musick. I told him that it affected me to such as degree, as often to agitate my nerves painfully, producing in my mind alternative sensations ... so that I was ready to shed tears ... [or] rush into the thickest part of battle. "Sir (said he,) I should never hear it, if it made me such a fool."'

11 For an account of the strong and weak imagers, see Berman, Introduction 2005 and 2008.

BIBLIOGRAPHY

Abbott, T. K. (1864), *Sight and Touch: An Attempt to Disprove the Received (Berkeleian) Theory of Vision*, Longman, Green.

Ayer, A. J. (1936), *Language, Truth and Logic*, Gollancz.

Berman, D. (1974), 'Hutcheson on Berkeley and the Molyneux Problem', *Proceedings of the Royal Irish Academy*.

Berman, D. (1994), *George Berkeley: Idealism and the Man*, Oxford University Press.

Berman, D. (1997), *Berkeley: Experimental Philosophy*, Phoenix Paperback.

Berman, D. (2005a), *Berkeley and Irish Philosophy*, Continuum.

Berman, D. (2005b), 'Berkeley: The Man and His Works', *Cambridge Companion to Berkeley*, edited by K. Winkler, Cambridge University Press.

Berman, D. (2008), 'Philosophical Counseling for Philosophers: A Confession of Images', *Philosophical Practice*.

Berman, D. (2013), 'Why Early Atheists Loved Berkeley's Idealism', *Le Cabinet du Curieux: Festschrift for J-P Pittion*, edited by M. Kosluk and W.K. Pietrzak, Classiques Garnier.

Unpublished works by Berman, but available as attachments by writing to the author, dberman@tcd.ie.

(2009) 'Manual of Experimental Philosophy'

(2010) 'Penult'.

(2015) 'Plato's Seventh Letter and the Artisan Workbook Method in Philosophy'.

(2016) 'The Logic, Evidence and Credibility of Genuine Reincarnation: [an edition of McTaggart's 1915] *Human Immortality and Pre-Existence* with introduction, commentary, notes and variant readings.'

Descartes, R. (1984), *The Philosophical Writings of Descartes*, 3 vols. Translated and edited by J. Cottingham, D. Murdoch, R. Stoothoff, Cambridge University Press.

Drury, O'C. (1996), *The Danger of Words and Writings on Wittgenstein*, edited by D. Berman, M. Fitzgerald and J. Hayes, Thoemmes Press.

Fraser, A. C. (1891), 'Visualization as a Chief Source of Psychology of Hobbes, Locke, Berkeley and Hume', *American Journal of Psychology*.

Galton, F. (1883), *Inquiries into the Human Faculty and Its Development*, reprinted 1907, J. M. Dent.

Hill, James (2021), 'Berkeley on Ideas and Notions', *The Oxford Handbook of Berkeley*, edited by S. C. Rickless, Oxford University Press.

Hume, D. (1739 and 1740), *Treatise of Human Nature*, (1967) edited by L. A. Selby-Bigge, Oxford University Press.

Hume, D. (1748), *Enquiry Concerning Human Understanding*, 2007, edited by Peter Millican, Oxford University Press.

James, W. (1904), 'Does Consciousness Exist?', *Journal of Philosophy*.

Kant, I. (1781), *Critique of Pure Reason*, translated and edited by N. Kemp Smith, (2006) Macmillan.

Kant, I. (1790), *Critique of Aesthetic Judgment*, translated by J. C. Merideth, (1911) Clarendon Press.

Kant, I. (1798), *Anthropology from a Pragmatic Point of View*, translated and edited by Robert Louden, 2006, Cambridge University Press.

Leibnitz, G. (1898), *Philosophical Writings*, edited and translated by Robert Latta, Clarendon Press.

Locke, J. (1690), *Essay Concerning Human Understanding*.

Luce, A. A. (1945), *Berkeley's Immaterialism*, Nelson and Sons.

Luce, A. A. (1949), *Life of George Berkeley*, Nelson and Sons.

Luce, A. A. and Jessop, T. E. (1948-1957), *Works of George Berkeley*, 9 volumes, Nelson and Sons.

McTaggart, J. (1915), *Human Immortality and Pre-existence*, Edward Arnold.

McTaggart, J. (1917), 'Personality', *Encyclopedia of Ethics and Religion*, edited by Hastings.

Montaigne, M. (1993), 'Friendship', in *Essays: A Selection*, edited and translated by M. A. Screech, Penguin.

Moore, G. E. (1903), 'Refutation of Idealism', Mind: A Quarterly of Philosophy and Psychology.

Moore, G. E. (1921), Review of Russell's *Analysis of Mind*, *Times Literary Supplement*.

Plato (1997), *Complete Works*, edited by John M. Cooper, Hackett.

Russell, B. (1912), *The Problems of Philosophy*, Home University Library.

Schopenhauer, A. (1819), *The World as Will and Idea*, (1997) edited by D. Berman, translated by J. Berman, Everyman.

Spinoza, B. (1677), *Ethics* and 'Correction of the Understanding' (1993), edited and translated by G.H.R. Parkinson, Everyman.

Warnock, G. (1953), *Berkeley*, Penguin.

INDEX